OPEN DOORS

The Young Professional's Guide to Mastering Emotional Intelligence, Communication, and Networking to Turn Talent Into Career Success

---

DR. KESTER CROSSE

TIA Publishing, LLC

© 2026 Dr. Kester Crosse

All rights reserved.

Published by TIA Publishing, LLC

No part of this book may be reproduced, distributed, transmitted, or stored in any form or by any means, without the prior written permission of the author, except for brief quotations used in reviews or scholarly works.

Disclaimer

The information contained in this book is provided for educational and informational purposes only. While every effort has been made to ensure accuracy, no guarantees are made regarding completeness or applicability. The author is not engaged in rendering legal, financial, medical, or professional advice. Readers should consult qualified professionals before applying any information contained herein.

Neither the author nor the publisher shall be held liable for any loss, damage, or injury resulting directly or indirectly from the use of this material.

Printed in the United States of America

Dedication

This book is dedicated to my ancestors and yours, whose choices, sacrifices, and quiet determination paved the way for the opportunities we now have. They worked so we could dream bigger, reach higher, and become our best selves.

To my grandparents, Winston and Iris Crosse, who made the brave decision to leave Trinidad in 1957 and come to America in search of better opportunities for their children.

To my grandparents, Charles and Annie Upshur, born in Virginia, who walked from Accomack County to southern Delaware in search of work on a chicken farm, believing that honest labor could build a better future.

To my parents, Kester Crosse Sr. and Gloria Upshur, whose daily sacrifices and unwavering faith gave my sister and me the chance to become more than we imagined.

I also dedicate this book to the named and unnamed—those who choose to lift others as they climb. We might not know every name, but we recognize their impact. Remember them. Honor them. Let their discipline and drive inspire your own journey.

This book is dedicated to my family, friends, their children, your family, your friends, and anyone dedicated to improving their ability to connect with others and create opportunities through relationships.

There are ten things that require no talent but can shift the course of your life: punctuality, work ethic, effort, body language, energy, attitude, passion, being coachable, doing extra, and being prepared.

You are the result of sacrifice. Now be the reason someone else rises because you refused to close the door behind you.

May the words in these pages not only open doors in your life, but also grant you the character and conviction to hold those doors open long enough for others to walk through as well.

Foreword

I have spent over three decades working with young people in communities and classrooms, on university campuses, and with experienced professionals in boardrooms and throughout corporate America's communications, government affairs, and philanthropy pipelines. Over the years, I have encountered business professionals who looked perfect on paper—impressive titles, exceptional credentials, flawless résumés—yet something vital was missing. At the same time, I have seen others, sometimes with fewer advantages and fewer titles, rise quickly because they understood something that cannot be learned in a classroom alone.

They understood people.

This book captures that truth with clarity, courage, and confidence.

My journey with Kester started in the summer of 1981 when we met as wide-eyed teenagers at a camp in Wilmington. From that sunny July forward, our lives became connected through almost every milestone of adolescence—long days at Haynes Park, late nights with friends in our Northside neighborhood, shared struggles at school, and the thrill of early achievements and wins. As our families became extensions of each other, I got to see firsthand the discipline, intelligence, and generous spirit that later defined his leadership and influenced his career path.

Over more than forty years, I have been lucky to call Dr. Kester Crosse my best friend, brother, and confidant. Long before his degrees, titles, and accolades, he had a rare ability to uplift others and deeply connect with people of all ages. That ability—to make individuals feel seen, heard, and valued—is the true mark of a leader that goes beyond just credentials.

Kester's unwavering dedication to improving the lives of those around him, his empathy, and his talent for genuine connection are qualities that cannot be fully captured by academic records or professional honors alone. These same qualities now define Dr. Crosse's work and voice in these pages. As you continue reading, you will discover not only a medical professional with an excellent bedside manner but also a leader whose authenticity inspires trust and whose example has impacted many lives—including my own, as he motivated me to pursue higher education with purpose and confidence.

What Dr. Crosse explains in this book is something many professionals learn too late, often after missed opportunities and unnecessary setbacks: success does not depend solely on talent. It depends on trust. It depends on presence. It depends on clear, confident communication. It depends on how you make people feel long before you ever demonstrate what you know.

What makes this book stand out is that it is based on experience rather than theory. It draws from real decisions, actual environments, and genuine consequences. Dr. Crosse knows what it's like to navigate spaces where expectations are high, margins are tight, and perception is as important as performance. More importantly, he knows how to prepare young people to enter those spaces confidently, rather than hesitating.

Part of that understanding was shaped by powerful examples in our neighborhood—especially my father, known to many as "Big Rick." He was, and remains, an influential force in the community where Kester and I grew up. Big Rick taught us how to walk into a room as if we belonged, how to make and hold eye contact, how to speak our names boldly and with pride, and how to carry ourselves with confidence. He was a steady presence—trusted, respected, and consistent. Whether cheering at basketball games and track meets or stepping in with guidance and discipline when needed, he modeled leadership through daily action. In ways he may never have realized, he helped shape future influencers, including Dr. Crosse, by reinforcing confidence, accountability, and the power of communication.

This is not a book about changing who you are.

It is a book about sharpening how you show up.

Building on the foundation of lived experience and earned wisdom established here, Dr. Crosse now invites you to step through the first open door—where connection becomes intentional, presence becomes powerful, and opportunity begins to take shape.

Rick Deadwyler

Corporate Affairs Executive

Contents

Prologue	1
1. Success in the Making	5
Why People Skills Matter More Than Ever	
2. Work Ethic	17
Lessons from Sports, Culture, and Community	
3. Phone Etiquette in a Digital World	27
The Silent Signals Adults Notice (And Never Mention)	
4. Your Story Is Your Résumé	39
Emotional Intelligence and the Power of Self-Awareness	
5. Do You Have the TEEE?	49
Integrated Leadership EQ and the Score that Predicts Success	
6. Life Choices and Market Value	61
How Emotional Intelligence Shapes Your Worth	
7. Mastering People Skills and Networking	75
The Cheat Codes No One Teaches You	
8. The Art of Small Talk	87
(Yes, It's a Skill)	
9. Communication That Opens Doors	97
How to Be Heard, Understood, and Remembered	
10. How to Start Cold Conversations	111
Without Fear or Awkwardness	
11. Career Pathways & Possibilities	127
Seeing Bigger, Reaching Further	
12. Running the Play	139
Putting It All Together	
Key Terms	149
Afterword	155
About the Author	161
References	163

Prologue

Occasionally, a book comes along that says out loud what many people have felt quietly for years. This is one of those books.

Too often, success is presented as a mystery-something reserved for the lucky, the gifted, or the well-connected. We are taught to chase grades, titles, résumés, and credentials, believing that if we stack enough achievements, doors will automatically open. For some, that works. For many others, especially young people navigating spaces where they are underestimated, it does not. What goes unspoken is that opportunity often moves through relationships, and relationships move through people skills.

This book tells that truth plainly and powerfully.

At its core, this is not just a book about communication, professionalism, or networking. It is a book about becoming aware of who you are, how you show up, and how your presence affects the rooms you enter. It is about understanding that success is not only about what you know or what you can do, but about whether people trust you, remember you, and want to see you win.

What makes this book special is that it speaks from lived experience rather than theory. The lessons here are grounded in real classrooms, locker rooms, boardrooms, clinics, conversations, and consequences. They reflect the realities many young African Americans face: being judged more quickly, watched more closely, and given less margin for error, while also refusing to accept limitations as destiny. Instead of asking readers to shrink or change who they are, this book teaches them how to translate their excellence in ways the world understands and rewards.

Throughout these chapters, you will see a consistent message: your story matters, your presence matters, and your choices matter. You will learn that work ethic is inherited but must be activated. That communication is not just about speaking, but also about listening, timing, tone, and awareness. Those phones, body language, and follow-up habits silently shape your reputation. Those cold conversations are not awkward interruptions but bridges to opportunity. And that careers are not accidents, they are pathways built step by step through preparation, courage, and connection.

Most importantly, this book does not talk *at* young people. It talks *with* them. It respects their intelligence while challenging their habits. It honors culture while emphasizing discipline. It balances confidence with humility, ambition with service, and excellence with responsibility. The message is clear: you do not need to wait to become impactful. You can start running the play right now.

This book is meant to be used, not just read. You will find assignments, reflections, and practical guidance woven into every chapter because growth requires action. If you apply what is written here consistently, you will notice something powerful begins to happen. People will listen to you differently. They will respond to you differently. They will see you differently. Not because you demanded respect but because you earned it through how you showed up.

Whether you are a high school student, a college student, a young professional, an athlete, an artist, or someone still figuring out your direction, this book meets you where you are and points you forward. It reminds you that success is not reserved for a select few. It is built daily by those who are intentional, prepared, and present.

As you turn these pages, read with openness and honesty. Reflect on how you show up. Notice which lessons challenge you. Those are often the ones that matter most. If even one chapter helps you open a door, strengthen a relationship, or believe more deeply in your own potential, then this book will have done its job.

Your future is not waiting for permission.

It is waiting for preparation.

This book is part of that preparation.

ONE

Success in the Making

WHY PEOPLE SKILLS MATTER MORE THAN EVER

Every generation has its moment. A stretch of time people later look back on and say: That is when things shifted. That is when new leaders emerged. That is when builders, thinkers, creators, and connectors stepped forward and reshaped what was possible.

Most people assume those moments belong only to history books, documentaries, or headlines. They believe success is something that happens to them, not something they actively build. They wait for the perfect time. They wait for a degree, a promotion, an invitation, a title, or for someone in authority to make it official.

That assumption quietly limits lives.

YOUR SUCCESS IS ALREADY IN THE MAKING

Here is what most people never realize early enough: you do not have to wait for success to happen. You do not need permission to become powerful. You do not need a platform to matter. Your success is already in the making right now, whether you are intentional about it or not.

Success rarely starts loud. It starts quietly. It is built on the decisions you make when no one is clapping. It is built in the work ethic you develop before anyone is watching. It is built in the way you treat people when you do not need anything from them. It is built into the habits you repeat long before they produce visible rewards. Success is not a single moment. It is a direction, and direction is chosen.

The first open door in life is understanding a simple but powerful truth: you are not just living through time, you are shaping your future. Every conversation you choose to engage in or avoid. Every habit you strengthen or ignore. Every relationship you build or neglect. Every opportunity you step toward or walk away from. Each decision becomes another brick in the foundation of your life. Some bricks make you stronger. Some bricks make you heavier. The only question is whether you are building on purpose.

PEOPLE SKILLS OPEN DOORS THAT TALENT ALONE CANNOT

This book is not about magic formulas, overnight success, or motivational hype. There are no shortcuts here. The foundation is a truth that almost no one explicitly teaches, yet everyone eventually learns the hard way: people skills open doors that talent alone cannot.

People often call them soft skills, but that label is misleading. These are power skills. They determine who gets access, who is trusted, who is mentored, who is invited back, and who is promoted.

What Is Emotional Intelligence (EQ)?

When I say 'people skills,' I mean what many call emotional intelligence (EQ). EQ is your ability to understand yourself, manage your emotions, read people accurately, and interact in a way that builds trust. EQ is how you carry yourself. It is how you communicate under pressure. It is how you respond when you are corrected. It is how you show respect without shrinking. It is how you make other people feel when they are around you. And in the real world, the way you make people feel becomes your reputation long before your résumé gets a fair look.

Psychologist and researcher Daniel Goleman, who helped bring EQ into mainstream leadership research, found that emotional intelligence is often more predictive of career success than IQ or technical skill, especially in roles that require collaboration, communication, and influence. His research with leaders across industries showed that EQ competencies were twice as important as cognitive ability for long-term performance and promotability.[i] A recent meta-analysis also found that emotional intelligence is significantly related to career adaptability, career decision-making self-efficacy, and overall career success across multiple industries and career stages.[ii]

WHY PEOPLE SKILLS MATTER MORE THAN EVER

That is why people skills matter more than ever. We live in a world where attention is fractured, and patience is short. People are distracted, guarded, overwhelmed, and constantly evaluating whether you bring peace or problems into their day. In that environment, the person who can communicate clearly, carry themselves confidently, listen well, show respect, and follow through becomes rare. And rarity creates value.

It does not matter if you are the smartest person in the room if you cannot connect. It does not matter if you have talent; if your attitude makes people avoid you. It does not matter if you are good if you are not memorable. Talent might get you noticed. People skills get you chosen.

I wrote this book because most young people are not taught how to navigate rooms full of opportunity. They are not taught how to introduce themselves with confidence. They are not taught how to read a room's energy, start conversations without anxiety, or build relationships with decision-makers. They are not taught how to follow up professionally, ask powerful questions, handle feedback without taking it personally, or make people feel respected and comfortable.

What Schools Don't Teach

Schools do a strong job teaching math, science, reading, memorization, and test-taking. They teach us what to think, but rarely how to interact. They prioritize knowledge over connection, information over communication, and grades over presence.

But the real world rewards a different skill set. It rewards people who can connect quickly, communicate clearly, show confidence without arrogance, handle conflict calmly, build trust over time, and make themselves easy and enjoyable to work with.

The Pattern I've Seen Repeatedly

I have seen this pattern repeatedly in medicine, business, sports, community leadership, and everyday life. I have watched two people with equal intelligence, equal work ethic, and equal credentials end up in completely different places. The difference was rarely raw talent. It was always communication. It was presence. It was emotional control. It was follow-through. It was how they made people feel. One person was technically strong but socially average. The other person was technically solid and socially excellent. The second person rose faster every time.

The world promotes people who can communicate. The world hires people who can connect. The world invests in people who have presence. And yet almost no one is taught how to develop these skills intentionally. That is why this book exists. It is a playbook for becoming the kind of person whose doors open and stay open.

Rick's Story: People Skills in Action

A close friend of mine, Rick, works for a Fortune 500 company. We have been friends since I was 11. He is the first person in his family to graduate from college and to rise to the Director of Government Affairs. He played Division 1 basketball at the University of Delaware and has outstanding people skills and a strong work ethic. People like him. People trust him.

One day, during a casual conversation, he said something that stuck with me. He said playing basketball taught him something most people never formally learn: how to show up in a team environment with accountability, communication, and pressure.

Sports teach people skills even when no one calls them that. Athletes grow up in environments where communication is demanded, accountability is expected, and conflict is unavoidable. They learn adaptability through travel. They learn emotional control through competition. They learn discipline through practice. They learn resilience through loss. They learn leadership through both winning and losing.

WHAT ATHLETES KNOW (AND EVERYONE NEEDS)

Rick said, when we see former athletes, we assume certain things. We assume they know how to show up. We assume they can talk to people. We assume they can handle pressure. We assume they know how to work.

Those assumptions matter because life often runs on assumptions. Long before someone sees your transcript or reads your résumé, they are forming conclusions based on your energy, your posture, your eye contact, your tone, and your ability to communicate with respect.

People skills make you promotable. A work ethic makes you dependable. Communication makes you noticeable. These are the same traits scholarship committees, hiring managers, investors, and organizational leaders evaluate, often without saying a single word about it. They are evaluating how you show up, not just what you can do.

The habits you build today quietly become your reputation tomorrow. If you are an athlete, the lessons you have learned on the court, field, track, or in the gym are already preparing you for life beyond sports. You have learned to wake up early, practice when you do not feel like it, listen to coaching, analyze mistakes without quitting, fight through fatigue, stay consistent, communicate in real time, and lead and follow as the moment requires. Those habits are transferable currency. They make you valuable in classrooms, workplaces, entrepreneurial spaces, leadership roles, and community settings.[iii]

TALENT OPENS THE FIRST DOOR – PEOPLE SKILLS OPEN EVERY DOOR AFTER

But here is the warning most young people never hear clearly enough: athletic ability can give you a head start, but people skills determine whether you keep that lead. Increasingly, opportunities that once felt automatic for athletes, such as internships, leadership positions, and professional connections, are being won by non-athletes who invested heavily in communication, networking, confidence, and personal development. Talent opens the first door. People skills open every door after that.

And if you are not an athlete, but a musician, artist, scholar, debater, creator, entrepreneur, or quiet high achiever, the same principle applies. Talent and hard work get you noticed. People skills get you selected. The world is full of gifted people who never rise because they never learned how to connect, communicate, and follow through. The world is also full of people with moderate talent who rise quickly because they are consistent, coachable, professional, and easy to trust. That is why people skills are not optional. They are leveraging.

YOU ARE COMPETING WITH THE INVISIBLE

Here is another truth most people learn late: you are competing with the invisible. Right now, somewhere across the country and across the world, another young person is preparing. They are attending leadership workshops, practicing communication skills, learning to network, building their résumé, intentionally seeking mentors, and mastering small talk and follow-up. You may never meet them. You may never see them. But you will compete with them.

Every opportunity you want has someone else quietly, consistently, and intentionally preparing for it. The difference between the person who gets chosen and the person who gets overlooked is rarely raw ability. More often, it comes down to who can hold a conversation, who introduces themselves clearly, who has presence, who follows up, who listens, and who makes others feel valued.

People hire the people they like. People promote those they trust. People mentor those they connect with. These outcomes are not accidents. They are skills.

That is why your EQ level starts with the decisions you make today. No one becomes successful in a single moment. Success is built through small, sometimes uncomfortable choices: making eye contact, shaking hands firmly, putting your phone away, speaking up, introducing yourself, practicing small talk, following up, choosing effort over excuses, choosing energy over apathy, and choosing to be coachable.

These choices feel ordinary. They feel small. They feel insignificant in the moment. But they are not. They are the beginning of your success story.

When people look back at your life, they may not remember the exact day everything changed, but you will. It will be the day you decide to take responsibility for how you communicate, how you show up, and how you treat people. That is the day people begin to see you differently. That is the day doors start opening. And the most powerful part is this: you are in complete control of that decision.

YOUR SUCCESS STORY STARTS TODAY

So, ask yourself honestly: what kind of success story do you want written about you? Not just what you want to achieve, but who you want to become while achieving it.

This book exists to teach the skills most people never learn. Skills that help you build genuine connections, communicate with confidence, navigate rooms full of opportunity, and become someone people want to say yes to. You do not need to wait for permission. You do not need to wait for a title. You do not need to wait for your moment.

Your moment can begin now. And your success story is ready to be written.

END-OF-CHAPTER ASSIGNMENT:

Before you turn the page, practice this out loud until it feels natural: a 15-second introduction with your name, where you are from, and what you are focused on right now. Then send one follow-up message today to someone you respect, such as a coach, teacher, mentor, supervisor, or professional. Keep it simple, keep it respectful, and do not overthink it. This is how doors begin to open, one intentional moment at a time.

i. Daniel Goleman, Emotional Intelligence: Why It Can Matter More Than IQ (New York: Bantam Books, 1995).
ii. Pirsoul, T., Parmentier, M., & Nils, F. (2023). Emotional intelligence and career-related outcomes: A meta-analysis. Human Resource Management Review, 33(3), 100967. https://doi.org/10.1016/j.hrmr.2023.100967
iii. Ernst & Young & espnW. (2022). Where will you find your next leader? The case for athlete-inspired leadership. EY Global. Retrieved from https://www.ey.com/en_au/athlete-programs/why-a-female-athlete-should-be-your-next-leader

TWO

Work Ethic

LESSONS FROM SPORTS, CULTURE, AND COMMUNITY

There is a rhythm to Black excellence. It is not rushed, but it is relentless. It is not loud, but it is undeniable. You hear it in the barbershop when debates slowly turn into lessons, when someone always knows the backstory and someone else reminds you why it matters. You hear it at family cookouts when elders sit back in folding chairs, laugh loudly, and then, without warning, start telling stories that sound casual but carry deep instruction. You feel it in church, in music, in the way voices rise and fall together, in caring, in struggle, in faith, and in resilience, all in the same breath.

You feel that rhythm when you step into a classroom, onto a court, into a band room, a choir stand, or a workplace aware, even if subconsciously, that you are not just showing up for yourself. You are carrying expectations. You are carrying legacy. You are carrying the invisible presence of generations who came before you and prayed for opportunities they never got to see.

As African Americans, many of us grow up understanding something powerful long before it is ever written in a book or explained in a lecture. We do not have the luxury of average. We do not have the luxury of "good enough." We must be excellent just to be equal and exceptional to rise. That truth is not meant to discourage you. It is meant to prepare you.

For our grandparents, excellence meant working jobs that broke their bodies and still showing up with dignity. It meant waking up before the sun, coming home after dark, and still finding strength to pour into their families and communities. For our parents, excellence meant breaking barriers in classrooms, offices, and neighborhoods that were never designed with them in mind. It meant over-preparing, carrying pressure silently, and learning how to succeed without being celebrated.

For you, excellence may look different, but it is no less demanding. Today, it looks like discipline. Presence. Communication. Emotional control. Consistency. The ability to connect with people who hold influence and open doors. The world may measure skill and talent, but our community has always measured something deeper: heart, hustle, and work ethic.

This chapter is about honoring that legacy, not as a burden, but as fuel and using it intentionally to build the future you deserve.

THE LEGACY OF WORK ETHIC IN BLACK CULTURE

Before you ever applied for a job or filled out a college application, there was already a work ethic inside you. It did not come from a textbook. It came from history. It was passed down through observation, example, and survival. While every culture carries discipline in its own way, this chapter speaks specifically from the African American experience, the one I know, the one that shaped me, and the one that continues to shape millions of young people navigating the same realities.

The African American work ethic comes from people who picked cotton under brutal conditions and still found joy in song. From women who cleaned houses and raised children not their own, so their own children could dream beyond survival. From men who worked in factories, railroads, and docks, knowing the system was stacked against them, but refusing to let bitterness steal their pride. From students who integrated schools where they were tolerated, not welcomed, and succeeded anyway. From families who worked twice as hard for half the recognition and still insisted on excellence.

This history is not trauma, it is power.

It is the source of a resilience that cannot be taught in workshops or motivational speeches. When you grind through a tough workout, push through fatigue, fight through doubt, or show up prepared when it would be easier not to, you are not doing it alone. You are tapping into a cultural memory of perseverance that has carried our people through centuries.

That is why effort matters. That is why discipline matters. That is why presence matters. You are never just representing yourself. You are representing every ancestor who often hoped, without evidence, that their descendants would go farther, live freer, and have more choices than they did.

SPORTS AS THE CLASSROOM OF DISCIPLINE

Step into almost any gym, field, track meet, or practice facility in our communities, and you will see a level of work that many adults would never voluntarily choose. Early mornings before school. Late nights after everyone else has gone home.

Repetition that looks boring to outsiders but builds muscle memory and mental toughness. Conditioning that leaves lungs burning and legs shaking. Film. Study. Feedback. Correction. Accountability.

Sports, especially in Black communities, have always been more than games. They have been classrooms. They have been proving grounds. They have been places where discipline was learned early because consequences were immediate. If you didn't show up prepared, it showed. If you didn't put in the work, the scoreboard told the truth. If you lacked effort, everyone could see it.

When people talk about a legendary work ethic, they often point to famous names. They talk about Kobe Bryant's "Mamba Mentality," but Black communities recognized that mindset long before it was branded. It is the same mentality that pushed Serena Williams to dominate entire fields that doubted her from day one. The same mentality that allowed Simone Biles to redefine a sport that was never designed for her body or brilliance. The same mentality that drives young stars today is showing up early, staying late, and mastering fundamentals long before the spotlight arrives.

Talent may bring you to the door. Work ethic keeps you inside. Consistency turns opportunity into legacy.

What many people miss is that this discipline does not disappear when the season ends. When transferred correctly, it becomes a professional superpower. Employers recognize it. Teachers sense it. Mentors invest in it. Leaders trust it. Work ethic is not loud, but it speaks fluently in every room that matters.

The Danger of Wasted Talent

Psychologist Angela Duckworth's research at the University of Pennsylvania found that traits like perseverance, consistency, and sustained effort were stronger predictors of long-term success than talent or IQ alone.[i] She calls this combination "grit," and her research confirmed what many elders, coaches, and communities have known for generations: talent may get you noticed, but work ethic gets you chosen.

This is one of the hardest conversations to have because it hits close to home. We all know someone who had "it." Natural ability. Swagger. Presence. Potential. They were the ones everyone talked about. The one who didn't have to work as hard to stand out. The one people assumed would "figure it out" eventually. Many successful people, including myself, were not the most talented, and we know of people who were more talented but did not do the actual work needed to succeed.

Potential is only a promise, not a guarantee.

Too many gifted young men and women miss opportunities because they rely solely on talent. Some assume scholarships will automatically appear. Others believe charisma will carry them. Some simply never realize how many people they are competing against, but who are preparing relentlessly.

The harsh truth is this: wasted talent is one of the most expensive losses in all communities, and the Black community is not immune.

African Americans cannot afford to waste what our ancestors sacrificed for. We cannot afford to let gifts go undeveloped because no one taught follow-through, communication, or consistency. We cannot afford another generation of brilliance that stalls not from lack of ability, but from lack of preparation.

This book is not here to shame you. It is here to protect you. It is your insurance policy against wasted potential.

 "If you don't know, now you know...."

Biggie Smalls

WORK ETHIC MATTERS MORE THAN EVER

In today's world, competition is wider and more invisible than ever before. You are not just competing with classmates or teammates. You are competing with students who attended leadership camps. with peers who had private tutors and early exposure to professional environments. With young professionals whose families already understand the unwritten rules. With people who have mentors making calls on their behalf.

Some of them start with more resources. That is real. But what remains true always is this: no one can outwork you without your permission.

I repeat...No one can outwork you without your permission.

When you combine Black resilience with strategic focus and strong communication, something powerful happens. You stop fitting into systems and start breaking molds. You become someone people watch closely. Someone leaders trust. Someone mentors advocate for. Work ethic, when paired with people skills, becomes leverage.

The Early-Morning Principle

Athletes understand something that transfers cleanly into every area of life: the advantage of being early. You wake up early to get extra shots in. You lift weights while others are asleep. You run drills before the day has time to distract you. That habit creates separation.

In life, early looks like being prepared before you are asked. It looks like arriving early to meetings. Early to opportunities. Early to follow up. Early to growth. The world notices people who show up early and with intention.

For Black professionals, consistency does more than advance individual careers. It quietly shifts expectations for everyone who comes after. When you show up early, prepared, and present, you reset the standard in spaces that may not expect it. That matters more than you may ever hear out loud.

The Community Is Watching

Every time you push through a hard moment physically, mentally, or emotionally, someone is watching. Younger siblings. Teammates. Cousins. Neighbors. Kids at the rec center see you walk by and imagine themselves in your place someday. They may never say it, but they study how you move, how you talk, how you respond to pressure, how you handle success and setbacks.

Your focus becomes their roadmap. Your work ethic becomes their blueprint. You become an example before you ever intend to. This is the soul of excellence. We rise not only to elevate ourselves, but so that others know that rising is possible.

YOU ARE YOUR OWN LEGACY

Work ethic is not something you turn on for special occasions. It is who you become through repeated choices. It is built quietly, reinforced daily, and revealed under pressure. When you commit to a focused life grounded in effort, consistency, communication, and presence, you honor the culture that raised you. You honor the barriers that were broken before you arrived. You honor the sacrifices your family made so you could have options.

Talent is God-given.

Work ethic is a choice.

Consistency is a lifestyle.

Excellence is our inheritance.

And now, it is your responsibility not to be perfect, but to be intentional. This is how legacies are built. Not loud. Not overnight. But relentlessly.

And now, it is your turn to choose outstanding focus and work ethic.

That intentionality starts with the thing closest to you right now — literally. The next chapter addresses the one habit that quietly tests your discipline dozens of times a day: your phone.

---

i. Angela Duckworth, *Grit: The Power of Passion and Perseverance* (New York: Scribner, 2016).

THREE

Phone Etiquette in a Digital World

THE SILENT SIGNALS ADULTS NOTICE (AND NEVER MENTION)

You just read about work ethic — the discipline your family modeled, the resilience your culture passed down, the daily decisions that separate those who rise from those who almost did. Now let me ask you a direct question: how much of that discipline disappears the moment you pick up your phone?

Your phone is powerful.

It can teach you.

It can connect you.

It can entertain you.

It can expose you.

It can distract you.

If you are not intentional, it can quietly destroy opportunities long before you ever realize they were available.

Phone etiquette is so poor today that you see more people doing it wrong at all ages, old and young. These devices are made to keep you on them by using addiction patterns, and their design is working. People are often not present in public. Most young people believe their phone habits are private. They are not. Adults, leaders, coaches, professors, managers, and mentors form opinions in seconds based on how you manage your phone in social and professional spaces. Those opinions often go unspoken, without feedback or a second chance to correct the impression.

I am placing this chapter early in the book for a reason. Before we talk about your story, your communication, your networking, and your career — all of which are coming — we need to address the one habit that silently undermines everything else. You can have the best introduction in the room, the strongest handshake, the most impressive résumé — but if your phone is in your hand when it should not be, people will form an opinion about you before you ever open your mouth.

In a world that values speed, access, and visibility, phone etiquette has become as important as communication, networking, and work ethic. Not because phones are bad, but because how you use them signals maturity, awareness, discipline, and respect. This chapter is not about demonizing technology. It is about helping you use your phone in a way that elevates your reputation instead of quietly limiting it. The people who get this will excel. Those who don't will be behind, but they won't know it since they will be behind where they would have been. They may be a manager, but with phone EQ, they would have been a VP.

YOUR PHONE IS ALWAYS COMMUNICATING

Every time you pull out your phone in the presence of others, you are communicating something, whether you mean to or not. You may think you are just checking a message or scrolling for a second, but to the person across from you, your behavior sends a message.

It can say, "I'm not fully present."

It can say, "This moment isn't important."

It can say, "I'm disengaged."

It can say, "I don't know how to interact without a screen."

Even if none of that is true, perception becomes reality.

In African American culture, presence has always mattered. Our elders understood that how you showed up spoke louder than what you said. We were taught to speak when we entered a room, to look adults in the eye, to pay attention, and to show respect through behavior. Those lessons were not about control. They were about preparation. They were teaching us how to move in a world that would judge us quickly and sometimes unfairly.

Those values are not outdated. They are your competitive advantage.

HOW PHONE HABITS QUIETLY LOWER YOUR MARKET VALUE

Your reputation — what this book will later call your "market value" — is shaped by small, repeatable behaviors. Every day, people form opinions about your professionalism based on what they observe, not on what you intend. Phone habits are one of the fastest ways to raise or lower how people see you, without saying a single word.

Using your phone during meals is one of the clearest signals adults notice. When you are eating with others, especially elders, mentors, or professionals, and your phone is out, it signals poor manners and low social awareness. It communicates immaturity and disengagement. People may not correct you, but they will remember it, and they may quietly decide you are not ready for more serious spaces.

Having your phone out during conversations is another reputation killer. Even quick glances tell the person speaking to you that they do not have your full attention. It sends a message that you would rather be somewhere else. Connection can die instantly when someone feels ignored.

At networking events, phone use is especially damaging. Holding your phone makes you look busy, closed off, or uninterested. It creates a physical barrier between you and opportunity. People will walk right past you and talk to someone else who looks open and present. People rarely interrupt someone who appears to be occupied with a screen.

Texting during meetings, class, team discussions, or training sessions is another habit leaders notice immediately. Presence is associated with seriousness. Distraction is associated with unreliability. Even one glance at your phone can weaken your credibility.

Recent research studies by the U.S. Surgeon General and others (Kadylak et al., 2023) support this.[i] People report feeling less trust toward individuals who "phub" them (snub via phone use). Phone use during face-to-face interactions creates feelings of ostracism and reduces perceived connection quality. In other words, the behavior does not have to be rude to damage your reputation—people read distraction as disrespect.

Oversharing online is another silent destroyer of reputation. Posting every emotion, argument, reaction, and private moment signals poor judgment. The internet never forgets. Screenshots exist. People you will meet in the future will see versions of you that you forgot you posted.

None of these behaviors feels dramatic in the moment. That is why they are dangerous. They don't blow opportunities up loudly. They slowly erode trust.

PHONE HABITS THAT RAISE YOUR REPUTATION INSTANTLY

The good news is that small changes create immediate results. Simply putting your phone away around adults, mentors, and leaders signals maturity. Not facing down on the table. Not half out of your pocket. <u>Away.</u>

Keeping your phone out of sight during meals communicates professionalism and social intelligence. People notice, even if they don't say anything.

Eye contact has become rare. When everyone else is buried in their screens, the person who looks up stands out immediately. Presence attracts conversation. Presence invites trust.

Not recording every moment is another sign of emotional maturity. Some moments are meant to be experienced, not documented. Knowing when to be fully present instead of reaching for your phone shows awareness and discipline.

Using your phone with purpose rather than compulsion changes everything. Checking your phone deliberately instead of reflexively puts you back in control. You decide when technology serves you, instead of technology controlling your attention. Turning notifications off and checking your phone on your terms is a major change I make, and I strongly recommend you do the same. If it's important, they can call.

Lastly, protecting your digital image is also essential. Your online presence is part of your market value. Assume everything you post is permanent. Assume employers, coaches, scholarship committees, and mentors will see it. Use your platform to reflect confidence, intelligence, culture, joy, and ambition.

BLACK REALITY: WHY THIS MATTERS EVEN MORE

Let's be honest about something uncomfortable but real. Black students and young professionals are often judged faster and more harshly.

A distracted white student may be labeled unfocused.

A distracted Black student may be labeled disrespectful, unprepared, uninterested, or "a problem."

That is unfair, but it is real.

This is why phone etiquette matters even more for you. Presence protects you. Awareness protects you. Discipline protects you. Your behavior can either reinforce a stereotype or dismantle it completely.

When you are present, respectful, and attentive, you control the narrative. You replace assumptions with evidence. You force people to see you clearly.

Phone Etiquette in a Digital World • 33

Figure 1: The Impact of Phone Etiquette

Choosing Presence in a Distracted World

Presence is rare today. Most people cannot sit in silence. Most people panic when they do not have their phone in their hand. Most people are addicted to scrolling.

But presence changes everything.

When you choose presence, people trust you more. Relationships deepen. Mentors notice. Leaders respect you.

Opportunities open. Presence is professionalism. Presence is discipline. Presence is power.

The ability to be fully present is a skill, and like any skill, it improves with practice. Meditation can help you manage and improve your presence. Good mental and physical control is a good presence.

Knowing When the Phone Should Disappear

There is a simple rule that covers every situation: if someone is paying attention to you, you should not be paying attention to your phone.

Any moment where someone is speaking to you, teaching you, coaching you, advising you, sharing their story, or serving you is a no-phone moment.

That includes interviews, introductions, meetings, events, meals, church, performances, networking, team huddles, and any face-to-face conversation. Your phone should never receive your attention before people do.

TEXTING AND DM ETIQUETTE: WHERE OPPORTUNITIES ARE WON OR LOST

Texting feels casual, but it carries consequences. Keep messages short, clear, and professional when communicating with adults or mentors. Avoid slang in professional contexts. Avoid late-night messages. Give people time to respond; do not double-text.

Never ghost someone unless safety is an issue. Silence communicates disinterest or immaturity. Few things lower your value faster.

Do not argue through text. Conflict belongs in conversation, not emojis. Remember that tone is easily misread. A third of texts are misinterpreted. If something feels confusing, pick up the phone and call. Read this paragraph again.

SOCIAL MEDIA: THE PUBLIC RESUME YOU DIDN'T ASK FOR

Social media is permanent. Screenshots live forever. Your digital footprint is part of your résumé. Over 70% of employers use social media to research candidates before making hiring decisions. Content that demonstrates professionalism, communication skills, and positive character traits influences hiring outcomes.[ii]

Avoid posting content that reflects poor judgment, negativity, recklessness, or lack of self-control. Your social media should tell a consistent story: confidence, intelligence, ambition, culture, joy, excellence, and leadership.

People will judge you by it. You might as well make it work for you.

Your Phone Is a Tool, not a Trap

Your future success depends on how well you balance digital life with real life. Your phone can open doors. But used carelessly, it can close them just as fast.

When you choose presence over scrolling, connection over distraction, and discipline over impulse, you stand out immediately. You become trusted. You become memorable. You become respected.

In a world full of screens, the ones who choose presence become unforgettable.

And here is the deeper truth: presence is not just about what you stop doing. It is about what you start becoming. When you put the phone away, you make space — space to listen, space to connect, space to tell your story. In the next chapter, you will learn how to craft and carry that story with confidence. But none of it works without presence. Presence comes first. Your story comes next.

END-OF-CHAPTER ASSIGNMENT: THE 24-HOUR PHONE PRESENCE CHALLENGE

For the next 24 hours, commit to the following:

No phone at meals.

Phone in your pocket during conversations.

Face the phone screen down during class or meetings.

No scrolling while standing in line, say hello to someone instead.

No late-night emotional texting or posting.

At the end of the day, write down what felt different. Notice your focus. Notice your confidence. Notice how people responded to you.

---

i. Kadylak, T., Makki, T. W., Francis, J., Cotten, S. R., Rikard, R. V., & Sah, Y. J. (2022). Feeling ostracized by others' smartphone use: The effect of "phubbing" on social interaction. PMC/NCBI. https://pmc.ncbi.nlm.nih.gov/articles/PMC9285876/
ii. Jeske, D., & Shultz, K. S. (2023). Tools, potential, and pitfalls of social media screening: Social profiling in personnel selection. Journal of Management, 49(7), 2391-2421. https://doi.org/10.1177/10506519231199478

FOUR

Your Story Is Your Résumé

EMOTIONAL INTELLIGENCE AND THE POWER OF SELF-AWARENESS

Now that you understand how presence protects your reputation, it is time to give people something worth remembering. You may not realize it yet, but you already carry the most powerful tool you will ever use in life. It is not your GPA, your jump shot, your job title, your internship, or your follower count. It is your story. Your story is the one asset no one can copy, steal, dilute, or outperform you on. It is your unique fingerprint on the world, shaped by your family, your culture, your struggles, your victories, and the quiet moments that taught you who you are long before anyone was watching.

Long before people decide whether they trust you, mentor you, promote you, invest in you, or open doors for you, they are asking a silent question: Who is this person really? Your story answers that question faster and more honestly than any résumé ever could. A résumé tells people what you have done. Your story tells them why you did it, how you think, and who you are becoming. And in a world driven by relationships, perception, and trust, that difference matters more than most people ever realize.

In our community, storytelling is not optional. It is tradition. Wisdom has always been passed down through testimony rather than textbooks. Through church testimonies that reminded us that survival was not luck but faith. Through porch conversations where elders spoke plainly about life's rules. Through barbershop debates that blend humor, strategy, and truth. Through kitchen-table counseling and late-night talks after cookouts, the real lessons finally surfaced. Long before LinkedIn profiles and elevator pitches existed, we learned how to explain ourselves through story.

Your story is more than what you have done. It is who you are becoming. And when you learn how to communicate your story with clarity, confidence, and emotional intelligence, doors begin to open sometimes before you even knock.

My story: I was born in Wilmington, Delaware, to Kester Crosse Sr. and Gloria Upshur, both of whom strongly emphasized education. A's and B's were expected, and C's were not acceptable. I have a younger sister, and my parents' marriage ended when I was ten years old. My educational journey began in Catholic schools, continued at Hampton University, and culminated at the University of Maryland School of Medicine. Medical school was the most challenging academic adversity I faced, and Hampton University provided the foundation and tools that allowed me to persevere and succeed. I chose gastroenterology after residency because my grandmother died of colon cancer when I was sixteen, and this specialty gave me the opportunity to screen for and prevent the disease, work I find deeply rewarding. I entered private practice, became company president in 2012, and now serve as Vice President of Clinical Affairs for GastroHealth, a national organization that merged with my practice in 2021. In life and love, I was married once before my current marriage of more than twenty years. That first marriage at twenty-five resulted in one child and sparked a personal commitment to grow and improve in relationships. Through counseling, I gained deeper self-awareness, addressed personal challenges, and strengthened my ability to build healthy relationships. I remarried at age thirty-four, had two more children, and today I am driven by a passion for mentorship and investing in the next generation, using every opportunity to make people and my community better.

WHY YOUR STORY MATTERS MORE THAN YOUR RÉSUMÉ

Résumés list tasks. Stories reveal purpose. Résumés show what you did. Stories explain why you did it. Résumés describe skills. Stories communicate character. In theory, performance should speak for itself. It rarely does, especially for Black students and professionals navigating spaces where assumptions are made quickly, and context is often missing.

People want more than credentials. They want a connection. They want to understand what shapes you, what motivates you, and how you respond under pressure. They want to know whether you can be trusted, coached, relied upon, and respected. This is where emotional intelligence becomes critical.

Emotional intelligence, often called EQ, is the ability to understand yourself, manage your emotions, read others accurately, and communicate in ways that build trust rather than tension. Storytelling sits at the center of EQ. It is how you help others understand you without over-explaining yourself. It is how you humanize your excellence. It is how you create familiarity in unfamiliar rooms.

Most people panic when asked a simple but powerful question: "So tell me about yourself." They ramble. They undersold themselves. They overshare. Or they retreat into safe, forgettable answers that reveal nothing meaningful. But when you understand your story and the emotional intelligence behind it, you answer that question in a way that makes people lean in, listen closely, and remember you.

Your story is not random. It is a bridge connecting you to mentors, leaders, decision-makers, and opportunities aligned with who you truly are.

WHERE YOUR STORY REALLY BEGINS

Your story does not begin the day you were born. It begins with the people who shaped you before you even understood what shaping meant. It begins with the grandmother who worked double shifts so you could walk into school with confidence. With the uncle who pulled you aside and told you to keep your head on straight when the world tried to pull you sideways. With the mother who refused to let you quit, even when quitting felt reasonable. With the father, coach, or mentor who demanded excellence long before you believed you were capable of it.

It begins with teachers who saw something in you that you could not yet see in yourself. With neighborhoods that sharpened your instincts and taught you to be aware. With setbacks that humbled you and blessings that reminded you that you were not alone. These experiences did more than shape your circumstances. They shaped your emotional intelligence.

They taught you how to read tone before words. How to recognize danger and opportunity quickly. How to adjust without losing yourself. How to speak when necessary and stay silent when wise. How to observe before reacting. These are not accidental skills. They are emotional competencies developed through lived experience.

You gained resilience. You learned empathy. You developed intuition. You built cultural awareness. You cultivated hunger. None of these are weaknesses. They are assets. They are proof that you have been training emotionally long before anyone gave it a name.

Pain, Pressure, and Struggle: The Training You Didn't Know You Were Getting

In the African American community, adversity is not an occasional visitor. It is a teacher who arrives early and stays long. Many of the challenges you faced growing up were not fair, but they were formative. They taught you how to navigate multiple worlds without losing yourself. How to read rooms quickly. How to stay calm under pressure. How to advocate for yourself without burning bridges. How to stretch limited resources. How to keep showing up even when support was inconsistent.

These lessons build emotional endurance, the ability to remain grounded while navigating uncertainty. Employers crave it. Leaders rely on it. Mentors recognize it immediately. Yet many young Black professionals try to hide these parts of their story, believing they will be seen as weaknesses.

That is a mistake.

Your struggle is not your identity, but it is your training. It is evidence that you have already been tested. It shows that you can adapt, learn, and grow. When framed with emotional intelligence, your story becomes proof of strength rather than a confession of hardship. The key is not what you went through, but what you learned and how it shaped the way you show up now.

SELF-AWARENESS: THE FOUNDATION OF A STRONG STORY

You cannot tell your story well if you do not understand it yourself. Self-awareness is the foundation of emotional intelligence. It is the ability to step back and recognize your patterns, triggers, strengths, blind spots, and values. Without self-awareness, storytelling becomes either bragging or apologizing, neither of which builds trust.

A strong story is grounded, not defensive. Confident, not arrogant. Honest, not raw. It reflects reflection. It shows growth. It signals maturity. Self-aware people do not need to exaggerate or hide. They communicate calmly because they know who they are.

When leaders hear someone speak with self-awareness, they relax. When mentors hear clarity, they lean in. When decision-makers hear the word 'purpose,' they invest. Self-awareness turns your story from noise into signal.

YOUR STORY HAS THREE PARTS: PAST, PRESENT, AND PURPOSE

Emotionally intelligent storytelling is structured, intentional, and concise. Whether you are in an interview, a scholarship conversation, a networking event, or a casual introduction, clarity matters. Think of your story in three parts: past, present, and purpose.

Your past is where you come from. This is not about trauma or oversharing. It is about the foundation. The values, environment, or early experiences that shaped how you think and work. You might say, "I grew up in Baltimore, where hard work wasn't optional; it was survival. My family taught me to show up early, listen closely, and take pride in everything I touch."

Your present is who you are today. This grounds your story in the now. It includes your current roles, interests, and strengths. "Today, I'm a student focused on leadership development, communication, and preparing for a career in healthcare. I'm intentional about growth and service."

Your purpose is to decide where you are going. This is the most important part. Purpose signals direction, values, and vision. "My goal is to become a physician and mentor young students the way others poured into me. I want to create access and opportunity for the next generation."

When you organize your story this way, people quickly understand you. They remember you longer. And they see where you are headed, which makes them more likely to help you get there.

Carrying Your Story with Pride

One of the greatest emotional intelligence challenges for Black professionals is learning not to shrink. Too many spend years minimizing the very things that make them powerful: their family, their culture, their neighborhood, their accent, their resilience. You may see these things as ordinary because they are familiar. Others often see them as extraordinary because they reflect depth, perspective, and lived experience.

 Your story is not a burden. It is currency.

Not a disadvantage, a differentiator. Not a limitation, a launchpad. When you own your story, your posture changes. Your voice steadies. Your introductions become intentional. Your confidence becomes quiet but firm. People feel it immediately.

Emotional intelligence is not pretending to be someone else. It is understanding who you are and communicating with control and pride.

The Moment Your Story Changes Everything

At some point, often sooner than you expect, someone will ask a question that determines your next opportunity: *"So tell me about yourself."* Most people are unprepared for this moment. They talk for too long. They talk too little. They apologize for ambition. They shrink.

But you will be ready.

When you speak your story with confidence and emotional intelligence, three things happen immediately. People trust you because clarity builds credibility. People remember you because stories stick. People want to help you because purpose invites investment.

Storytelling is a superpower in every field of business, sports, medicine, entrepreneurship, and leadership. For African Americans, it provides context for excellence. It reframes assumptions. It replaces stereotypes with substance. You are not a statistic. You are not a résumé. You are a story and a powerful one.

Your story is not something you prepare once and put away. It is something you carry with you into every interaction. It is the foundation of networking, the fuel of cold conversations, and the reason people remember you after the moment passes. Before you exchange contact information, before you ever follow up, before you ever ask for guidance or an opportunity, people are listening to your story, even when they don't realize it.

In Chapter 7, you'll learn how people skills turn conversations into relationships. In Chapter 10, you'll learn how to start conversations with confidence when you don't know anyone at all. But both of those skills depend on this one truth: if you don't know your story, you won't know what to say when the moment matters most.

END-OF-CHAPTER ASSIGNMENT: WRITE YOUR STORY

Take ten uninterrupted minutes and write three sentences.

Where I come from: *"My childhood taught me _____."*

Who I am now: *"Today, I am a person who _____."*

Where I am going: *"My purpose is to _____."*

These are not final drafts. They are foundations. You will refine, shorten, and adapt them for different rooms. But once you know them, you will never be caught off guard again.

Crafting your story is the first act of emotional intelligence. It is the first act of leadership. It is the moment you stop waiting to be understood and start communicating intentionally.

Your story is your résumé.

And when you learn to tell it well, the world listens.

FIVE

Do You Have the TEEE?

INTEGRATED LEADERSHIP EQ AND THE SCORE THAT PREDICTS SUCCESS

Early in my leadership journey, I ran into a problem that many leaders experience but few stop to question. We were evaluating people year after year using the same tools: generic categories, vague descriptions, and checkboxes that encouraged safe, noncommittal answers. Every evaluation looked the same. Most people were rated "average" or "above average," and yet the outcomes told a very different story. Productivity varied widely. Morale fluctuated. Some individuals carried teams while others quietly stalled progress. None of that showed up clearly on paper.

WHY TRADITIONAL METRICS MISS THE MARK

I remember reviewing those evaluations and feeling deeply unsatisfied. They didn't tell me who was truly effective. They didn't tell me who needed coaching. They didn't help me identify future leaders. And most importantly, they didn't help people grow. The process felt more about avoiding discomfort than creating clarity. Everyone left with a decent score, but nothing changed.

That frustration forced me to step back and ask a more honest question: How do you measure effectiveness? Not potential. Not intention. Not personality. Effectiveness.

The answer didn't come from a leadership seminar or a management textbook. It came from sports.

Growing up around sports teaches you one undeniable truth: the score is the score. It does not matter how hard you tried, how talented you are, or how good you look warming up. When the game ends, the scoreboard tells the truth. It is objective. It is honest. And it is final. That clarity is what sports get right and what leadership evaluations often miss.

So, I decided to bring that same clarity into leadership.

Like most data-driven leaders, my first instinct was to go straight to numbers. Productivity. Output. Results. Metrics matter, and they always will. But as I studied performance more closely over time, another truth emerged, one that surprised me. Talent alone did not predict success. Some of the most gifted hires never became top performers. Meanwhile, others with modest résumés and average credentials consistently outperformed everyone around them.

That observation raised a bigger question: What separates the average from the outstanding?

I began paying closer attention not just to what people produced, but to how they showed up. I listened to how they spoke. I observed how they handled pressure, feedback, conflict, and responsibility. I watched what happened when things went wrong. I tracked patterns over months and years, not days or weeks. Slowly, a framework emerged. Something consistent. Something measurable. Something predictive.

Eventually, I gave it a name.

THE TEEE SCORE.

TEEE might look simple. But once you understand it, you start seeing it everywhere in high performers, in leaders you admire, and in moments when people either rise or stall. The TEEE Score captures what traditional evaluations miss: the why behind success. It explains why some people with obvious talent plateau while others with fewer advantages accelerate. It measures behaviors that create trust, momentum, and opportunity over time.

TEEE gave me something I never had before. It gave me a way to measure intangibles with the same clarity as a scoreboard. It created a fair and objective framework that reduced bias and favoritism. It helped predict long-term success, not just short-term impressions. And it transformed how teams were built and coached.

Performance was no longer about popularity, tenure, or gut instinct. It became about behaviors tied directly to outcomes. People understood what was expected. Leaders knew what to coach. High performers finally had language for what they were already doing right. And once you understand TEEE, you begin to see why people with high TEEE always succeed regardless of raw talent alone.

Every leader evaluates people, whether they admit it or not. Coaches, managers, principals, executives, and mentors all carry internal scorecards. They may not call it TEEE, but the questions they ask are remarkably similar.

When a coach evaluates a player, four questions usually guide the decision-making process. First, talent: Can they do it? Do they have the baseline skill to compete? Second, effort: Do they want it? Are they willing to work, practice, and push through discomfort? Third, energy: Do they lift the team up? Do they bring presence, positivity, and emotional engagement? Fourth, execution: Do they deliver when it matters? Can they translate preparation into results?

Employers ask the same questions using different language. They want to know who can perform, who can be trusted, who elevates the culture, and who gets things done. Most people believe success is about peak moments, the highlight reel, the big win, the standout performance. TEEE is about what you do consistently. Consistency becomes your reputation. Reputation becomes your opportunity. Leaders do not promote potential forever. Eventually, they promote patterns.

Figure 2: The four components of the TEEE Score

The TEEE Score consists of four components. Each one matters individually, but the real power is in how they work together.

T — Talent: What You Can Do

E — Effort: How Hard You Work When No One Is Watching

E — Energy: How You Make People Feel

E — Execution: Your Ability to Deliver Results

Talent is your starting point. It represents what you can do with your skills, knowledge, intelligence, and natural abilities. Talent gets you noticed, but it does not keep you chosen. Talent without follow-through quickly becomes frustrating to leaders. Everyone has seen the "high potential" individual who never quite delivers.

 "Talent opens doors, but it does not keep them open."

Effort is your engine. It reflects how hard you work when no one is watching. Effort shows up in preparation, persistence, discipline, and willingness to improve. Leaders notice effort because effort is contagious. More importantly, effort signals coachability. You can teach skills. You cannot teach hunger.

Energy is how you make people feel. This is where emotional intelligence lives. Emotional intelligence impacts leadership effectiveness, team performance, and organizational outcomes.[i] Energy includes attitude, presence, communication, emotional awareness, and engagement. High-energy individuals attract opportunity because people enjoy being around them. They make work feel lighter. Low-energy individuals drain rooms even when they are talented. Energy determines whether people lean in or pull away.

Execution is delivery. It is the ability to deliver results in real-world conditions. Execution means finishing strong, meeting deadlines, following through, and performing under pressure. Execution is where credibility is built or lost. Leaders forgive mistakes. They do not forgive patterns of non-delivery.

Most people are strong in one or two of these areas. Very few are strong in all four. Those who have become indispensable.

In conversations with CEOs, business owners, coaches, and hiring managers across industries, I hear the same message repeated: talent is common; reliability is not. Degrees are everywhere. Certifications are abundant. Résumés are polished. What leaders are searching for is someone they can trust to show up, contribute, and deliver consistently.

When someone demonstrates high TEEE, momentum follows naturally. People talk about them in rooms they are not in. Opportunities appear without chasing. Coaches trust them with responsibility. Mentors invest time and guidance. Leaders advocate for them when decisions are made. High TEEE scores turn you from "someone with potential" into "someone who gets things done."

Your TEEE Score starts today. Not tomorrow. Not after another opportunity. Right now.

Take a moment and rate yourself honestly in each category on a scale from one to ten. You are not allowed to use seven. Seven is where honesty goes to hide. Rate your talent. Rate your effort. Rate your energy. Rate your execution. Scores of eight or higher indicate strength. Scores of five or six are average. Scores below five signal an area that demands attention. This exercise is not about judgment. It is about clarity. Honest assessments are needed.

A HIGH TEEE HIRE

When our company was preparing to expand, we opened a search for a new Chief Operating Officer. We hired a national recruiter, reviewed an impressive stack of résumés, and assembled a committee to lead the process. As president of the company, the final decision ultimately rested with me.

The candidate we selected surprised some people.

He was the youngest person we had ever hired for the role. He didn't have elite schools on his résumé. On paper, he wasn't the most credentialed candidate we interviewed.

What he *did* have was presence.

From the moment he walked into the building, his effort was unmistakable. He was prepared, engaged, and intentional with every interaction. His energy was contagious—staff members felt it immediately. By the end of the interview and site visit, people across departments independently told us the same thing: *"I like him."*

That reaction mattered.

He made everyone feel better at the end of the visit than they did at the beginning. That's not charisma—that's emotional intelligence paired with purpose. While other candidates may have had stronger résumés, no one delivered a better *experience*.

We hired him.

To this day, he remains the best leadership hire I have ever made. He executed at a high level, earned trust quickly, and elevated the people around him. His success wasn't driven by pedigree—it was driven by effort, energy, and execution.

Today, he serves as a Vice President at a major medical corporation, exactly where someone with a high TEEE score belongs.

HOW TO CALCULATE YOUR TEEE SCORE

Scoring overall is easy. 32 or better overall is very good. 20-32 is average. Scores under 20 mean a person needs work in every important area.

Everyone has gaps. High-TEEE individuals are not perfect; they are intentional. They are focused. They identify weaknesses and work on them deliberately. When your people skills catch up to your talent and effort, everything changes. Confidence grows. Relationships deepen. Opportunities multiply.

When you review your own TEEE score, you can focus deliberately on areas for improvement. When you review others' TEEE scores, you're better positioned to help them focus where it matters most.

Success is not one dramatic leap. It is the accumulation of small habits practiced with intention. Talent starts the journey. Effort keeps you moving. Energy attracts people and opportunity. Execution gets you across the finish line. Together, they create reliability, trust, and respect.

TEEE is not a label. It is a focus. And once you start living it, you will never look at success or yourself the same way again.

Let's keep building.

CHAPTER PRACTICE DRILL: RAISING YOUR TEEE IN REAL TIME

This chapter is not meant to be admired. It is meant to be applied. TEEE does not improve through intention alone; it improves through awareness and repetition. This drill is designed to help you identify where your TEEE is strong, where it leaks, and how to intentionally raise it.

For the next seven days, choose **one** TEEE category to focus on. Not all four. One. Each morning, write that category at the top of a page. Throughout the day, notice moments when that category is tested. If you choose effort, notice when you want to coast. If you choose energy, notice how your mood affects others. If you choose execution, notice how you finish tasks. If you choose talent, notice where skill development is needed.

Work on what needs work and focus on habits that make you better.

At the end of each day, answer this question in writing: What did I do today that raised my TEEE and what lowered it? Be honest. No judgment. Just clarity.

At the end of the week, review your notes and answer one final question: If someone scored my TEEE based on my last seven days, what would my score be?

TEEE improves when awareness turns into focused improvement in areas that matter most. Focus turns into consistency. And consistency is what changes trajectories.

That is how success becomes predictable.

---

i. Suárez-Albanchez, J., Gutiérrez-Broncano, S., Jiménez-Estévez, P., & Palacios-Florencio, B. (2023). Emotional intelligence, leadership, and work teams: A hybrid literature review. Heliyon, 9(10), e20356. https://doi.org/10.1016/j.heliyon.2023.e20356

SIX

Life Choices and Market Value

HOW EMOTIONAL INTELLIGENCE SHAPES YOUR WORTH

There is a phrase you hear often in business, sports, and entrepreneurship: your market value.

WHAT IS MARKET VALUE?

It is usually spoken in the language of contracts, salaries, draft picks, and negotiations. People talk about who is "worth" what, who is overpaid, underpaid, or undervalued. But market value is not limited to money, titles, or transactions. It applies to life itself. It shows up in how people respond to you, how they trust you, how they open doors for you, and how they remember you when you are not in the room. Your market value is shaped every day by the choices you make, the habits you build, how you regulate your emotions, and how you carry yourself into every space you enter.

Big Rick: A Lesson in Presence

As a young man, I was blessed to have strong male role models, men who were not perfect, but who were present. One of those men taught me a lesson that has stayed with me for decades. He taught me about *presence*, how you show up when you arrive. His name was Big Rick, and the name fit him not because of his size, but because of his energy. Of note, Big Rick was the father of my best friend, Rick. I saw Big Rick up close since I was 11 years old. Big Rick did not have a prestigious job title. He was a medical supply deliverer by trade. Yet when he walked into a room, people felt him. They listened. They respected him. They made space for him. His job did not define his market value. His presence did.

Big Rick showed up with confidence, but not arrogance. He spoke calmly, but firmly. He made eye contact. He listened more than he talked. He treated everyone with respect, whether they were the CEO or the kid sweeping the floor beside him. He had standards for himself, and people could feel that immediately. Watching him taught me something powerful at a young age: how much people believe you are worth is often based on how you show up long before they know anything else about you.

Market value, in its simplest form, is this: it is how much people believe you are worth based on your presence, behavior, and emotional intelligence. That belief forms quietly. Long before a résumé is reviewed. Long before an interview. Long before a recommendation is written. Your market value is being shaped in everyday moments, the ones most people underestimate or dismiss as insignificant.

MARKET VALUE IS BUILT IN SMALL MOMENTS

Here is a truth many young people never hear clearly enough: your market value is being built long before you ever sign a contract, accept a job, or step into a leadership role. It is built by your daily choices. The small ones you think do not matter.

The habits you repeat without thinking. The way you handle frustration. The way you communicate when you are tired, stressed, or under pressure. Emotional intelligence is the engine behind all of this. It is not just about being "nice" or "calm." It is about awareness, discipline, regulation, and intention.

For African American students and young professionals, understanding market value is especially critical. Too many doors have historically been closed to us for reasons that had little to do with talent and everything to do with perception, communication, and presentation. This chapter is not about changing who you are to please others or shrinking yourself to fit into uncomfortable spaces. It is about understanding how value is perceived so you can move with intention, protect your opportunities, and choose your path rather than have it chosen for you. That understanding is power.

Many people believe opportunity begins the moment someone notices them. They think the right person must see their talent, discover their potential, or stumble across their work. But the truth is the opposite. Opportunity begins when you start making decisions as if someone is watching, even when no one is. Market value is not built in dramatic moments. It is built quietly, consistently, and privately.

It is built when you choose to study rather than scroll endlessly on your phone. When you arrive early, instead of sliding in at the last minute. When you look people in the eye instead of looking down at a screen. When you listen fully instead of mentally rehearsing what you want to say next. When you follow up without being reminded. When you do work, even when you are tired. When you choose integrity over shortcuts. When you communicate clearly instead of assuming people "should know." These moments may feel small, but they stack.

Over time, they form patterns. And patterns become reputations.

Emotional intelligence lives inside these choices. It shows up in your ability to delay gratification, regulate your emotions, read the room, and act with intention rather than impulse. You are not only being evaluated when you are formally evaluated.

You Are Always Being Observed

You are being observed all the time. That reality is not meant to create anxiety. It is meant to create awareness. When you understand this, everyday life becomes an opportunity to raise your value rather than something that just happens to you.

In the real world, impressions are formed quickly. Energy, communication, consistency, and emotional maturity are often noticed long before credentials are verified. Leaders are rarely asking only, "Can this person do the job?" They are also asking, "Can I trust this person? Do I enjoy working with them? Do they make things easier or harder?" These questions are not written on performance reviews, but they drive decisions behind closed doors.

WHAT RAISES YOUR MARKET VALUE

Your market value rises when people describe you as reliable, easy to work with, thoughtful, disciplined, and emotionally steady. When they notice that you communicate clearly, accept feedback without becoming defensive, follow through on commitments, and carry yourself with confidence. These comments may never be written down, but they travel quickly through conversations. People talk. And once a reputation forms, it is hard to reverse.

Your market value drops just as quietly. It drops when people notice that you do not listen, that you are always distracted, that you are late, defensive, disengaged, or inconsistent. These behaviors often feel small to the person displaying them, but they compound rapidly in others' minds. Every interaction either adds to your value or discounts it. There is no neutral. The question is not whether people are judging you. The question is whether your choices are increasing or decreasing the associations people have with your name.

THE CULTURAL DIMENSION: WHY THIS MATTERS MORE FOR US

For African Americans, there is an added layer that must be acknowledged honestly. In many spaces, you may be the only Black student, the only Black intern, the only Black athlete on scholarship, the only Black manager, or the only Black voice at the table. That reality carries weight, whether anyone says it out loud or not. When you walk into those rooms, you are often representing more than just yourself. You may be representing your family, your neighborhood, your school, or an entire community to people who lack exposure or understanding.

It is not fair, but it is real. And pretending it does not exist does not protect you from its effects. This is why market value has a cultural dimension for us. It does not mean you have to be perfect. It means you must be purposeful. Our families have always understood this. That is why certain phrases were repeated growing up: "Don't embarrass me in public." "Carry yourself with pride." "Give them nothing bad to say about you." "Whose child are you?" "Don't let anyone outwork you." These were not just sayings. They were survival tools passed down by generations who understood that perception could open doors or close them permanently.

When authenticity is paired with strong communication, discipline, and emotional control, something powerful happens. Stereotypes begin to break. Expectations are disrupted. People see someone who leads with intention, sets standards, and creates a sense of comfort and trust in unfamiliar spaces. That is Black excellence in practice, not as a slogan or a hashtag, but as a lived discipline.

BEHAVIORS THAT RAISE YOUR VALUE

Certain behaviors raise your market value everywhere you go. Respect is foundational. How you treat people who cannot help you says more about your character than how you treat people who can. Janitors, assistants, receptionists, cafeteria staff, and security guards notice how you treat them. And they talk. Respect has a way of circulating back to you, often when you least expect it.

Coachability is another powerful value booster. People who listen, who can receive feedback without shutting down or becoming defensive, rise quickly. Leaders enjoy investing in people who are open to growth. Being described as someone who listens is one of the highest compliments you can receive. It signals humility, maturity, and emotional intelligence.

Strong communication raises your value immediately. Speaking clearly, making eye contact, shaking hands with confidence, and articulating your thoughts show self-respect and respect for others. It tells people you take yourself seriously, without needing to dominate the room. Consistency builds trust. Showing up prepared, focused, and engaged creates reliability. Leaders trust what they can predict, and trust creates opportunity.

Self-control is a quiet form of leadership. Not reacting emotionally, not escalating conflict, and not taking everything personally demonstrate maturity. Emotional regulation is one of the clearest markers of high EQ. Hard work without constant complaint is rare and deeply admired. People notice who grinds without needing applause. Responsiveness also matters more than most people realize. Returning calls, replying to emails, and following up communicates professionalism. Silence often communicates indifference, even when that is not the intention.

BEHAVIORS THAT LOWER YOUR VALUE

On the other hand, some habits quietly lower your market value. Being constantly on your phone signals boredom, insecurity, or disrespect, regardless of your actual intent. Chronic lateness erodes trust faster than anything else. It communicates that your time matters more than others'. Poor attitude shows quickly through body language, eye-rolling, sighing, or visible frustration. Disappearing when things get difficult is unforgettable. People remember who shows up under pressure and who does not.

Defensiveness blocks growth. If people feel they cannot correct you, they will stop investing in you. Inconsistency erodes credibility. Doing something well once and disappearing is often worse than never doing it at all. Reliability is built through repetition. Your value does not drop because of who you are. It drops because of how you show up.

MARKET VALUE IS NOT FIXED

One of the most empowering truths about market value is that it is not fixed. It is flexible. It is not permanently tied to your past mistakes. It responds quickly to intention and consistency. You do not need perfection to raise your value. You need discipline. Start doing small things well, consistently, and your value rises. Stop doing small things poorly, and opportunity begins to appear.

Even if you mishandled opportunities before, you could rebuild starting today. Emotional intelligence allows growth. Your value is not defined by where you started, but by how you respond, adjust, and mature. Life is not random. You do not rise by accident. You rise by choosing discipline over distraction, communication over silence, presence over phone use, humility over ego, growth over excuses, and preparation over panic.

These choices move you from potential to presence, from presence to impact, and from impact to influence. You are building your market value every single day—not to impress people, but to open doors for yourself, your family, and your future children. This is how generational wealth begins. This is how generational confidence forms. This is how generational opportunity is created.

Big Rick taught it to his kids, and he taught it to me. It starts with choices.

But Big Rick was not the only teacher in that household. His wife, Miss Paulette, modeled a different dimension of emotional intelligence, one rooted in kindness, emotional perception, and communication. She had a way of speaking to people that made them feel seen. When she asked how you were doing, you could tell she actually cared about the answer. She listened with her face, not just her ears. She could sense when someone in the room was uncomfortable, and she would adjust the environment to make them feel included. That kind of social awareness is subtle but powerful. It builds connection. It builds trust. It raises market value in every room it enters.

Together, Big Rick and Miss Paulette created an ecosystem where presence and kindness were not abstract concepts — they were daily expectations. Their daughters are proof of what that kind of environment produces. Their oldest daughter, Sheena, became a VP at a bank in Delaware, not simply because she was intelligent, but because she learned how to manage relationships, communicate clearly, and navigate rooms where emotional intelligence mattered as much as technical skill. Their younger daughter, Ashley, became a dynamic business leader known for lighting up a room, putting people at ease, and communicating in a way that energizes others. Those outcomes were not accidental. Children rarely learn emotional intelligence from lectures; they learn it from observation, repetition, and exposure to adults who model it consistently.

People often assume EQ is innate, something you either "have" or "don't have." But environments teach it. Mentorship teaches it. Families teach it. And for those who did not grow up around it, books, mentors, coaches, classrooms, and deliberate practice can teach it too. Some learn these skills through lived experience. Others learn them later through reading, reflection, and intentional practice. The path is different, but the power is the same.

END-OF-CHAPTER ASSIGNMENT: BUILDING YOUR MARKET VALUE IN REAL TIME

This chapter is not meant to be read and admired. It is meant to be practiced. Market value is not built by understanding ideas; it is built by applying them consistently. This assignment is designed to help you become aware of how you show up, how you are perceived, and how your daily choices are shaping your value—often without you realizing it.

For the next seven days, begin by paying attention to your presence. Notice how you enter rooms, how you sit, how you listen, and how often you are distracted by your phone. Observe your body language, your eye contact, and your tone when you speak. Do not try to change everything at once. Simply become aware. Awareness is the first skill of emotional intelligence, and you cannot improve what you do not notice.

At the end of each day, write a short reflection answering this question: If someone had to describe my presence today in one sentence, what would they say? Be honest. This is not about self-criticism; it is about clarity. Over the course of the week, patterns will begin to emerge. Those patterns are your current market value in motion.

Next, identify three small choices you make repeatedly that either raise or lower your value. These might include punctuality, responsiveness, phone use, listening habits, follow-up, attitude under stress, or how you speak to people who cannot help you. Write about when these behaviors show up and what triggers them. Understanding your triggers is a key part of emotional intelligence.

Then, choose **one** behavior that lowers your market value and commit to changing it for the next fourteen days. Not five behaviors. Not a complete personality overhaul. One intentional adjustment. If it is late, commit to arriving 10 minutes early. If it is phone distraction, commit to keeping your phone away during conversations. If it is defensiveness, commit to listening fully before responding. Small, consistent improvements compound faster than dramatic promises.

Finally, answer this question in writing: What kind of reputation do I want my name to carry when I am not in the room? Do not write what sounds impressive. Write what feels true. Then ask yourself whether your current daily choices align with that reputation. If they are not, identify what needs to change and why.

This assignment is not about becoming someone else. It is about becoming more intentional about who you already are. Market value grows when emotional intelligence turns awareness into action. Do this exercise honestly, and you will begin to feel the shift—not just in how people respond to you, but in how you see yourself.

That is where real growth begins.

Midbook Review

The first half of this book introduces a simple but powerful truth: talent alone is rarely enough. The professionals who consistently advance are those who understand people, communicate with intention, and cultivate authentic professional relationships.

If the insights in this book have already provided value, consider taking a moment to leave a brief review on **Amazon**. Your feedback not only helps other readers discover the book, but it also supports the broader mission of equipping young professionals with the tools they need to grow, lead, and succeed.

If you would like to explore additional resources or stay connected with Dr. Kester Crosse, visit **drcrosseauthor.com**. The website provides updates, insights, and future content designed to help you continue building the professional skills and relationships that open doors throughout your career.

As you continue reading, consider how the principles introduced so far apply to your own professional journey—and how you can begin putting them into practice.

SEVEN

Mastering People Skills and Networking

THE CHEAT CODES NO ONE TEACHES YOU

If talent and work ethic get you on the field, and your story gives you identity, then people skills are the secret sauce that gets you invited into rooms money cannot buy. This is the part of success that feels invisible until you understand it—and then you start seeing it everywhere.

Not everyone has a 4.0 GPA.

Not everyone is a star athlete.

Not everyone grows up with family connections or professional access.

But absolutely everyone can learn people skills.

That is why these skills matter so much. They are not reserved for the privileged, the extroverted, or the naturally charismatic. They are learnable, repeatable, and transferable. And once you master them, they change the trajectory of your life.

Here is the secret most people never hear early enough: people skills beat talent when talent cannot connect. People skills beat intelligence when intelligence cannot communicate. People skills beat privilege when privilege cannot relate.

In our community, many of us were not formally taught these skills at home or in school. That gap is not your fault. But closing it is your responsibility, and doing so will change everything about how the world responds to you.

This chapter breaks down the cheat codes.

Before I break down the cheat codes of people skills, I will share something personal. Medical school early years were tough. The written years and data years were very tough and have nothing to do with people skills. However, once I moved into my clinical years, I found that people skills matched with intelligence made me excel in a space where connecting with people, identifying what is wrong, and communicating effectively are hallmarks of a high-level physician. Strong people skills do not require a test, so they play no role in the early years of medical school, but having them changed my medical career trajectory from just being a good physician to being a good leader of physicians and physician groups. Connecting, or networking, well, is critical to your journey to success.

WHY NETWORKING IS NOT "BEING FAKE"

One of the biggest mental blocks young people, especially young Black men and women, have about networking is this fear of being fake. You hear it all the time. "I don't want to sound like I'm trying too hard." "I don't like talking to strangers." "I don't know what to say." "That feels fake to me."

Let's clear this up immediately.

Networking is not being fake. Networking is being intentional.

It is not pretending to be someone you are not. It is learning how to show people who you already are in a way they can understand, remember, and trust. Networking is not about using people. It is about building relationships that grow over time.

Networking is simply the process of creating opportunities through connections. It is how jobs happen. It is how internships happen. It is how scholarships happen. It is how mentors appear. It is how doors open quietly, without announcements.

You have been networking your entire life; you just never labeled it that way. When someone at church takes a liking to you and introduces you to someone else, that is networking. When a coach connects you with a former player or a colleague, that is networking. When an elder at a cookout pulls you aside and says, "Come here, I want you to meet someone," that is networking.

Networking is not a business activity. It is a life skill. I have a good friend who has a very high TEEE score and outstanding people skills. He was smart in college, and his talents included intelligence, work ethic, and people skills. He was a biology pre-med major in college, but it was not in his heart. Medicine was not his passion. He found his passion in sales and using his people skills. He works today in wealth management, which combines his high TEEE skills with the sale of a lucrative product. He can network with the best of him and has mastered his intelligence and people skills to become very successful.

The Truth: People Like People Who Are Easy to Talk To

Your greatest opportunities will not come from online applications alone. They will not come from random luck. They will not come from being "discovered" while sitting quietly and hoping someone notices your talent.

They will come from relationships.

Someone says your name in a room when you are not there. From someone recommending you because of how you made them feel. From someone trusting your character before they analyze your résumé.

People open doors for people they like, respect, and feel comfortable with. They open doors for people who are kind, confident, attentive, and warm. They open doors for people who listen, who communicate clearly, and who make interactions feel easy rather than awkward.

In every industry, medicine, sports, business, education, tech, and entrepreneurship, leaders are constantly looking for people they can trust and connect with. Skills matter, but relationships decide access.

If someone enjoys talking to you, they are far more likely to help you.

Networking Facts No One Teaches Young People

Research shows that employee referrals are 4x more likely to result in a job offer than online applications, and referred candidates stay at companies significantly longer (Zippia, 2023).[i] Networking is not a luxury skill — it is how opportunity actually moves in the real world, often quietly and through people long before announcements are made.

Author Keith Ferrazzi, whose research focuses on high-performance social capital, notes that your success is heavily influenced by the strength of your relationships and the quality of your collaborations, not just your credentials. [ii]

People hire whom they trust, promote whom they connect with, and mentor those who show humility and effort. Networking simply makes those connections visible.

There are realities about opportunity that rarely get explained clearly enough. Most jobs and internships are filled through relationships, not job boards. Most opportunities come from positive impressions made long before formal decisions are announced.

Quiet confidence beats loud arrogance every time. Consistency beats flash. Respect beats bravado.

And here is one of the most important truths: people open doors for people who remind them of their younger selves. They help people they see potential in, people they connect with emotionally, and people whose stories resonate with their own journey.

That is why your story, your presence, and your communication matter so much.

THE FROM METHOD: A SIMPLE CONVERSATION SYSTEM THAT WORKS EVERYWHERE

One of the biggest reasons people struggle with networking is that they do not know what to say. When nerves kick in, minds go blank. That is why you need a system.

Figure 3: The "FROM" method.

The **FROM** method is one of the simplest and most effective conversation frameworks you will ever use. It works in professional settings, social events, networking functions, conferences, and casual gatherings.

F stands for From and for Family. People love talking about where they are from and who matters to them. Asking about family creates warmth immediately.

R stands for Recreation. What someone does for fun tells you who they are outside of work or school. Hobbies humanize conversations.

O stands for Occupation. This is where professional interests come in, but framed in terms of curiosity rather than interrogation. For young people, this can be their college major and the subjects they are interested in.

M stands for Motivation. This is where conversations deepen. Asking what drives someone or what they are working toward builds real connection. Finding a person's passion and what drives them can build even a deep connection.

You do not need to ask every question. You simply move naturally through the framework. FROM keeps conversations flowing and removes pressure. This one skill alone can change your confidence forever in connecting with people.

HOW TO START A CONVERSATION WHEN YOU FEEL NERVOUS

Most people wait too long to speak because they think they need the perfect opening line. You do not. You need a respectful one.

Simple introductions work. Saying your name clearly matters. Asking how someone is connected to an event always works. Commenting on something you genuinely notice, a jacket, a comment they made, or a role they mentioned opens doors naturally.

Compliments open doors when they are sincere. Respect keeps doors open. Confidence brings you inside.

The goal is not to impress. The goal is to connect.

Presence, Eye Contact, and Nonverbal Communication

What you say matters, but how you show up matters more. People feel your energy before they process your words. Your posture, eye contact, facial expressions, and attentiveness communicate far more than your vocabulary.

Nonverbal communication tells people whether you are confident, respectful, engaged, and professional. In our community, presence has always been currency. We know how to walk into rooms with dignity. The key is learning to apply that same awareness in professional spaces.

When you walk into a room, walk in like you belong and not like you are intruding. Belonging is not about entitlement. It is about self-respect.

Your Presence Speaks Before Your Words

Before you say a single thing, your body and energy introduce you. Adults are watching. Leaders are watching. Coaches are watching. They are looking for eye contact, posture, a real handshake, a genuine smile, calm energy, politeness, and gratitude. Those signals communicate, "This young person is serious."

Don't shrink your body to make others comfortable. Don't talk to the floor. Don't rush your words like you're apologizing for taking up space. Stand tall. Keep your shoulders relaxed. Let your voice come from your chest. Make eye contact. Smile lightly. Speak clearly. Own your space. You belong in every room you're in. You don't need permission to be present.

For African American students, presence matters even more because people sometimes misread you before they know you. Your calm, respectful confidence protects you. It shapes perception before stereotypes have room to form. When you show up regulated and intentionally, you control the narrative.

Phone Etiquette: A Fast Way to Raise or Lower Your Value

Your generation is judged heavily by phone behavior. Fair or not, this is reality. How you use your phone around others sends loud messages. As we discussed in Chapter 3, proper phone etiquette can help you tremendously — and in a networking setting, it matters even more.

Scrolling while someone is speaking signals disinterest, disrespect, or insecurity, even if that is not your intention. Keeping your phone away during conversations, meals, and networking events communicates presence and professionalism immediately.

When opportunity shows up, your phone should be invisible.

This alone will separate you from most people your age.

Listening Is More Impressive Than Talking

One of the most underrated people skills is listening. Not waiting to talk. Not planning your next response. Listening fully. God made you with two ears and one mouth, so you should listen twice as much as you talk.

Listening communicates maturity. It shows confidence. It signals respect and intelligence. When you listen well, you make the other person feel valued, and that makes you memorable. Listen: maintaining eye contact while listening helps with connections.

 People remember how you made them feel long after they forget what you said.

People remember if you listened to them, since many do not listen and just wait to talk.

THE FOLLOW-UP: WHERE MOST OPPORTUNITIES ARE LOST

Meeting someone once is not networking. Following up is networking.

Most students never follow up. They assume the moment passed. It did not. The moment begins with a follow-up. Most people don't follow up.

A simple thank-you message within 24 hours sets you apart immediately. Mentioning one specific thing you learned shows attentiveness. Expressing interest in staying connected keeps the door open.

This habit alone places you in the top tier of young professionals.

Your Network Is Your Safety Net

In our community, we have always relied on the village. No one succeeds alone. You need a network that includes mentors, teachers, coaches, professionals, alumni, peers, and younger students you can guide.

A strong network protects you, supports you, teaches you, and opens doors your résumé cannot.

Most successful Black professionals have a village behind them. You are building yours now intentionally.

END-OF-CHAPTER ASSIGNMENT: START BUILDING TODAY

This week, introduce yourself to an adult who can help you grow. Send one follow-up message. Practice the FROM method with one new person.

Networking is not a personality trait. It is a skill.

And now, you have the cheat codes.

The next chapter will show you how to speak with confidence every time you open your mouth and how to command respect without raising your voice.

You are not late. You are learning exactly on time.

---

i. Zippia Career Research. (2023). Employee referral statistics: How referrals impact hiring. Zippia Research. Retrieved from https://www.zippia.com/advice/employee-referral-statistics/

ii. Keith Ferrazzi, *Never Eat Alone: And Other Secrets to Success, One Relationship at a Time* (New York: Crown Business, 2005).

Forrier, A., De Cuyper, N., & Akkermans, J. (2024). The role of social capital in employability models: A systematic review. Sustainability, 17(5), 1782. https://www.mdpi.com/2071-1050/17/5/1782

Mobley, S. D., & Johnson, J. M. (2024). The HBCU advantage: Reimagining social capital among students at historically Black colleges and universities. Frontiers in Education, 9, 1344073. https://doi.org/10.3389/feduc.2024.1344073

EIGHT

The Art of Small Talk

(YES, IT'S A SKILL)

If networking is the doorway to opportunity, then small talk is the key that unlocks it.

Most people never think about small talk this way. They treat it as background noise, filler conversation, or something to endure until the "real" conversation starts. Some even dismiss it as pointless, awkward, or unnecessary. That misunderstanding costs people opportunities every single day.

SMALL TALK IS THE KEY TO OPPORTUNITY

Small talk is not about the topic. It is about the connection. It is the warm-up before the relationship, the handshake before the mentorship, and the conversation before the opportunity. Small talk is how people decide whether they feel comfortable with you, trust you, and want to continue engaging with you. Before résumés are reviewed and credentials are discussed, people form an impression of you. Small talk is where that decision begins.

If you have ever watched seasoned politicians work in a room, you have seen small talk at a master level. They know how to lock in with someone for three minutes or thirty minutes, just long enough to create a connection, build favor, and establish trust. They do not rush. They do not dominate. They listen, respond, and make people feel seen. That skill is not accidental. It is training.

WHY SMALL TALK MATTERS MORE FOR US

Mastering small talk matters for everyone, but for young African American students and professionals, it is especially powerful. Small talk gives you confidence in unfamiliar spaces. It gives you control over first impressions. It allows you to move smoothly into rooms where you may be the only one who looks like you. It helps you turn everyday moments into bridges instead of barriers. In spaces where assumptions already exist, small talk becomes a tool for shaping narrative and perception.

This chapter is about removing anxiety from conversation and replacing it with ease. It is about understanding that small talk is not something you are either "good at" or "bad at." It is a skill. And like any skill, it improves with understanding and practice.

My Fellowship Interview: Connection Changed the Outcome

I learned this firsthand during my fellowship interviews. My ability to make genuine connections through conversation played a major role in earning my position. I was told that the department chair had not hired an African American fellow during his tenure. That information did not change my approach. I did not need him to agree with me or see the world my way. I needed him to connect with me as a person, and he did.

The interview began awkwardly. Early on, I was asked, "When did you first know anyone white?" That question could have derailed many capable people in this interview setting, and understandably so, but I had bigger goals. I relied on emotional intelligence and connection rather than reaction. I answered calmly, "Second grade. Sister Joan was my math teacher. She was a wonderful person." He followed up by asking if I had attended Catholic school. I told him I had for ten years and that it had been a great experience. He shared that he had also attended Catholic schools, and suddenly the conversation shifted. We talked about school, structure, and even Mass.

Later, he apologized for the question and explained that seeing my HBCU background on my CV made him curious about my exposure to white culture prior to medical school. That interaction is not the point of this book, but it is an example of how people skills help you reach your goals. I was offered the fellowship and became the first African American male fellow in his department. We went on to have a strong professional relationship. Connection changed the outcome and opened a door for me on my journey towards success.

MOST OPPORTUNITIES START IN ORDINARY MOMENTS

Most major opportunities do not start with dramatic speeches or formal interviews. They start quietly, often in moments that feel insignificant at the time. A brief conversation before a meeting. A hello in the hallway. A comment while waiting in line. A short exchange before class or practice. A casual introduction that begins with, "You two should meet." These moments rarely feel important when they happen, but they are exactly where impressions are formed.

What often separates successful people from everyone else is not that they talk more. It is that they know how to turn small moments into meaningful connections. They understand that opportunity often comes wrapped in ordinary interactions. The world opens for people who know how to talk not in a performative way, not in a fake way, but in a confident, comfortable, human way. Small talk is how people decide whether to lean in or pull back, whether to engage or disengage, whether to remember you or forget you.[i]

BLACK CONVERSATION IS ALREADY A CULTURAL SUPERPOWER

There is also something powerful that often gets overlooked: Black conversation is already a cultural superpower. We talk well. We always have. Conversation is embedded in our culture. We know how to laugh, tease, vibe, ask questions, tell stories, and make people feel seen. We grew up around aunties who could talk for hours and still remember every detail. Uncles who knew everyone's nickname. Barbershop debates that felt like ESPN mixed with life coaching. Cookouts where conversations jumped from sports to politics to family in minutes.

We are raised in environments where reading energy is survival, not theory. Knowing when to speak, when to listen, and when to joke matters. Where connection is currency. The issue is not that you do not know how to talk. The issue is that no one taught you how to translate that natural ability into professional and academic spaces. No one explained that the same skills you already have just need to be polished, slowed down slightly, sharpened, and redirected.

THE GOAL OF SMALL TALK: COMFORT, NOT PERFECTION

The goal of small talk is not perfection. It is comfort. People remember how you made them feel long after they forget what you said. If you make someone feel comfortable, you become memorable. Comfort creates safety. Safety creates connection. When people feel at ease around you, conversation flows. When they feel judged, rushed, or pressured, conversation shuts down. Small talk sets the emotional tone for everything that follows.

How to Start Small Talk

Starting small talk does not require clever lines or perfect timing. It requires presence. One of the easiest ways to begin is to comment on the shared moment you are both experiencing. The environment gives you material for free. An event, a class, a long line, the energy in the room, these neutral observations lower pressure. Noticing someone's style choices rather than commenting on their body also works well. Shoes, a jacket, a bag, or a watch are safe, respectful entry points. Asking simple questions removes performance pressure. Light humor, when used naturally, signals humanity.

Confidence is not loudness. It is calm energy. When you start conversations with ease, people mirror that ease back to you.

YES-ADD-ASK METHOD

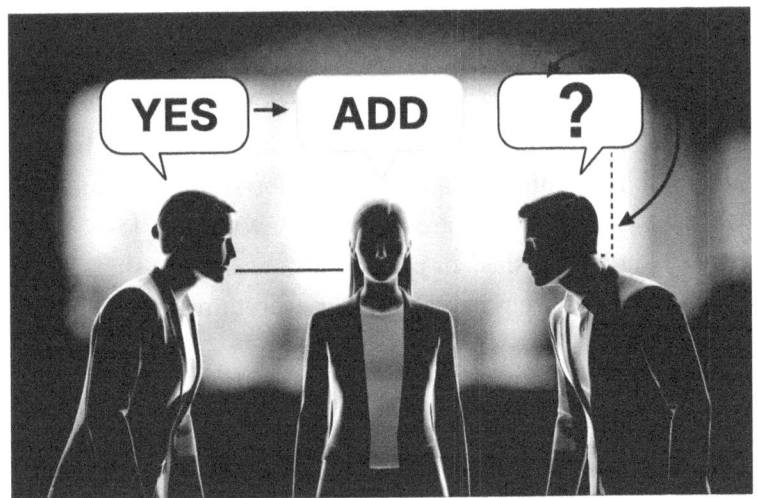

Figure 4: The "Yes-Add-Ask" technique.

When conversations feel dry, structure helps. The **YES → ADD → ASK** method is one of the most effective conversation tools you can use for conversation.

Yes - You acknowledge what was said.

Add - You add one related thought.

Ask - You ask a follow-up question. This creates rhythm without interrogation or monologue.

For example, if someone says, "I'm majoring in biology," you might respond, "That's a strong major. I've seen many biology students go into healthcare or research. What made you choose it?" Flow happens naturally. The pressure disappears.

Rules for Strong Small Talk

Strong small talk also follows a few standing rules: eye contact, light smiles, nodding, letting people finish, keeping your phone away, and genuine curiosity. These small behaviors separate people who merely talk from people who connect.

HOW TO END CONVERSATIONS WITH GRACE

Ending conversations well matters just as much as starting them. A clean exit leaves a positive final impression and keeps doors open. You do not need excuses or awkward apologies. Appreciation plus clarity is enough. Saying, "I really enjoyed talking with you, let's stay in touch," communicates confidence and respect. Never disappear mid-conversation. Strong communicators know how to exit with grace.

Black culture is built on warmth, rhythm, and authenticity. When you bring that energy into professional spaces with polish and awareness, you stand out. People do promote résumés, but they also promote energy. They mentor people they enjoy. Small talk builds familiarity. Familiarity builds trust. Trust creates opportunity.

Small talk is not small. It is big. It is the beginning of a big part of your success journey.

END-OF-CHAPTER ASSIGNMENT : THE SMALL TALK PRACTICE DRILL

Reading about small talk will not make you good at it. Practicing it will. Small talk is not a personality trait. It is a muscle. And like any muscle, it strengthens through repetition.

This assignment is designed to remove pressure and build confidence in real-world settings. You are not practicing to be impressive. You are practicing to be comfortable.

For the next seven days, commit to one intentional conversation per day. Not long. Not deep. Just intentional. On Day One, practice presence by making eye contact and offering a clear, confident greeting to someone you would normally pass by.

On Day Two, offer a respectful compliment on someone's style choice.

On Day Three, ask one FROM question and listen fully.

On Day Four, use the YES → ADD → ASK rhythm in a real conversation.

On Day Five, have an interaction with no phone visible.

On Day Six, end a conversation intentionally and confidently.

On Day Seven, reflect in writing on one awkward moment, one natural moment, and one surprise.

Do not judge yourself on outcomes. You are doing training reps, not collecting validation. Awkward moments mean growth is happening. Silence means learning. By the end of the week, small talk will feel less forced, your body language will relax, your anxiety will drop, and your presence will increase.

You will not become perfect.

You will become comfortable.

And comfort is what opens doors.

---

i. Methot, J. R., Rosado-Solomon, E. H., Downes, P. E., & Gabriel, A. S. (2021). Office chitchat as a social ritual: The uplifting yet distracting effects of daily small talk at work. Academy of Management Journal, 64(5), 1445-1471. https://doi.org/10.5465/amj.2018.1474

NINE

Communication That Opens Doors

HOW TO BE HEARD, UNDERSTOOD, AND REMEMBERED

Communication is not just talking.

It is not just words.

It is not volume, vocabulary, or sounding impressive.

Communication is connection.

Communication is confidence.

Communication is an opportunity.

Every door you will ever walk through in life can be opened or quietly closed by communication. People may read your résumé, check your GPA, review your transcript, evaluate your talent, remember they also often experience how you communicate. They feel your presence. They sense your confidence. They decide, often subconsciously, whether engaging with you feels easy or uncomfortable, safe, or uncertain, promising or risky.

In today's world, where attention is fragmented and distractions are everywhere, strong communication has become rare. And because it is rare, it is powerful. For young African Americans in particular, communication is more than a soft skill; it is a protective skill, a differentiator, and an amplifier. It helps you to be understood instead of misread. It helps you be respected instead of underestimated. It helps you lead without raising your voice and stand out without performing.

This chapter will show you how communication works beneath the surface. Not just what to say, but how to say it. Not just how to speak, but how to be felt. When you master communication, you don't chase opportunity. Opportunity begins to recognize you.

WHY COMMUNICATION MATTERS MORE THAN EVER

Opportunities do not always go to the smartest person in the room. They do not always go to the most talented, the most credentialed, or the most accomplished on paper. More often, they go to the person who can communicate clearly, calmly, and confidently.

Leaders often choose people they feel comfortable talking to. Coaches trust players who can listen and respond. Teachers invest in students who engage respectfully. Employers promote those who can articulate ideas, take feedback, and represent the organization well. Mentors pour into young people who show emotional maturity and self-awareness through communication.

Strong communication helps get you hired because people trust clarity.

It helps get you promoted because people trust reliability.

It helps to build relationships because people trust how you make them feel.

It creates memory because people remember presence.

Here is the truth most people never say out loud: people rarely give opportunities to someone they do not feel comfortable communicating with. Discomfort shuts doors quietly. Comfort opens them consistently.

Your communication is your reputation in motion. It speaks for you when you are not in the room. It answers questions people never ask directly: Can I trust this person? Can I work with them? Will they represent me well? Will they handle pressure with maturity?

Whether you realize it or not, your communication is already opening or closing doors. This chapter is about helping you open more of them on purpose.

THE FOUR LEVELS OF COMMUNICATION

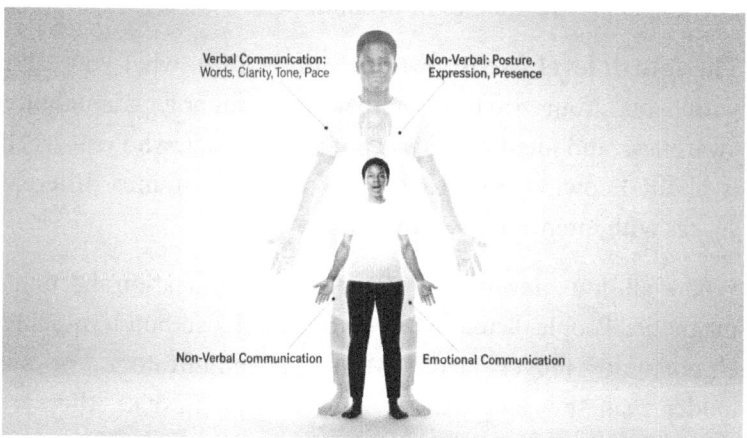

Figure 5: The Four levels of communication

Most people think communication is just verbal, what you say. Communication operates on four levels simultaneously, and people experience all of them whether they intend to or not.

The first level is verbal communication: your words, clarity, tone, and pace. This is the most obvious layer, but it is not the most powerful. You can say all the right things and still lose trust if the other levels are weak.

The second level is nonverbal communication: your posture, eye contact, facial expressions, body movements, and physical presence. Clothing, body art, and hairstyles. This level speaks before your mouth opens. People read your body language instantly, look at your clothes and body art, and decide whether to lean in or pull back.

The third level of communication is emotional communication: how you make people feel. This is your energy. How is your energy? Warmth, calmness, respect, openness, confidence, or tension all live here. This is where emotional intelligence comes into play. This is also where people decide whether they enjoy being around you. Positive energy people are good to be around.

The fourth level is cultural communication: what you carry with you. Your rhythm, authenticity, humor, adaptability, awareness, and identity. This is not about hiding who you are. It is about knowing how to bring your full self into different spaces with intention.

When all four levels are aligned, communication becomes magnetic. People listen without trying. Trust builds quickly. Opportunity moves faster. Master communicators are not louder than they are clearer. They are not flashier; they are steadier, with good communication across all four levels.

Verbal Skills: Sounding Prepared, Not Performed

This is a very important section. We talked about the 4 levels of communication.

Clear communication does not mean sounding "proper," "white," or unlike yourself. It means sounding prepared. Preparation communicates respect for yourself and for the person listening.

One of the most important verbal habits is pace and pitch. Speaking too fast signals nervousness or insecurity. Speaking too slowly can signal uncertainty. A steady, controlled pace and pitch with range communicates confidence and thoughtfulness. You cannot talk at the same pace and pitch since that is boring. Your goal is not speed. Your goal is clarity.

Finishing your sentences matters more than people realize. Trailing off at the end of statements sends a subtle signal of doubt. Ending your sentences with intention tells people you believe what you are saying.

Filler words "um," "like," "you know" are natural, but too many weaken your authority. They make you sound unsure, even when your idea is strong. Awareness is the first step to improvement. As your confidence grows, filler words fade.

Voice projection is not about yelling. It is about speaking from your chest instead of your throat. Chest voice sounds grounded and confident. Throat voice sounds tense and unsure. Relax your shoulders, breathe deeply, and let your voice settle.

Strong communicators use short, clear sentences. Clarity beats complexity every time. You do not need fancy language to sound intelligent. You need intentional language.

Finally, eliminate apology language from your everyday speech. Phrases like "Sorry for asking, but…" can usually be replaced with "Quick question…," which is more confident and effective. Saying "This might be dumb…" undermines you before your idea even lands. Instead, use phrases like "Here's what I'm thinking" or "Can I test an idea with you?" These communicate respect—without apology. Speaking with respect and confidence starts with believing in yourself and choosing the right words.

Non-Verbal Communication: What Your Body Is Saying

Your body speaks before your words do. People form opinions about you within seconds, often before you finish your first sentence. For young Black men and women, non-verbal communication is especially important because it can either elevate perception or be unfairly misinterpreted.

Eye contact communicates presence. Not staring, not intensely, just focused attention. It says, "I see you, and I'm engaged. Avoiding eye contact is often misread as disinterest, insecurity, or discomfort, even when that isn't the case.

Posture sets the tone for confidence. Stand tall, shoulders relaxed, head up. Slouching sends a message of uncertainty, even if you feel confident inside. Confidence often begins with your physical frame.

Visible body art communicates without a single word. Tattoos and body art can signal creativity, individuality, toughness, risk tolerance, or culture. The key is understanding the **setting**. In some spaces, body art makes people lean in. In other settings, especially among older generations or corporate audiences, the same body art can create distance or concern. A neck tattoo might say "bold" or "original," but in certain boardrooms, it may still say "not one of us," and you must know that before you walk in.[i]

This is not about right or wrong, it's about learning what unlocks opportunity. Expression matters. **But so does strategy.**

Handshakes still matter. A firm, warm handshake communicates professionalism and respect. Too aggressive, feels insecure. Too limp feels disengaged. First impressions are formed here more often than people admit.

Facial expression matters more than words. A relaxed face and light smile soften interactions and invite connection. Tension closes doors. Calm opens them. Never underestimate the power of a genuine smile to communicate confidence and approachability.

Movement communicates intention. Avoid fidgeting, pacing, or restless gestures. Move with purpose. Walk into rooms as if you belong — because you do. When your body is calm, people feel safe engaging with you.

Attire and grooming speak volumes. Clothes, hair, and accessories tell a story before you say your name. For young people, especially, there is a difference between how your peers read your style and how the people who control opportunities read it. The people who open doors, managers, owners, investors, directors, and professors are evaluating for trust, professionalism, and judgment.

Sagging pants on men may feel expressive among peers, but it rarely communicates competence or reliability to the people who write recommendations or extend internships. For women, overly sexualized attire may attract attention, but often the wrong kind of attention that ignores your intellect and undercuts your credibility. Neither is a fair measure of talent, but they affect perception.

Hair and hairstyles also communicate. Locs, braids, twists, fades, curls, these are powerful cultural expressions and should be embraced. Just understand what your hairstyle signals in a particular space and how to balance personal identity with professional intention. Expression with awareness is a superpower.

The goal is not to suppress identity. The goal is to be **strategic** about communication. Good eye contact, strong posture, a firm handshake, a warm face, intentional movement, and thoughtful presentation can open doors before you speak. The opposite can quietly close them.

At the end of the day, non-verbal communication shapes how you are perceived:

Do people like you? Do they trust you? Do they remember you positively?

Those three questions decide how many doors open for you and how fast.

Emotional Communication: The Energy You Bring

People don't just hear you. They feel you. "Vibe" is an important form of communication. It's an energy communication form.

Your emotional communication tells people whether you are kind or harsh, confident or defensive, coachable or rigid, grateful or entitled. This happens beneath language. It is your vibe, which is short for vibration.

Your tone matters. Your breathing matters. Your openness matters. When you are regulated emotionally, people relax around you. When you are reactive, people pull back.

Emotional intelligence is not about suppressing emotion. It is about managing it. It is about responding instead of reacting. It is about staying grounded under pressure. It's about being positive under pressure.

People rarely remember exactly what you said, but they remember how you made them feel. Emotional communication is often the difference between someone recommending you or forgetting you.

Your energy introduces you before your words do.

Cultural Communication: Power Without Disappearing

African American communication is rich, expressive, and powerful. Rhythm, warmth, humor, storytelling, adaptability, and emotional intelligence are strengths, not liabilities. Growing up in Wilmington, but attending white catholic schools taught me code shifting. It taught effective communication at the park in my neighborhood and in the school lunchroom.

Maturity in communication is not about changing who you are. It is about knowing how to shift your delivery without losing your identity. This is not code-switching. This is code-shifting.

Code-switching says, "I have to become someone else to be accepted."

Code-shifting says, "I am skilled enough to effectively communicate across environments while remaining myself."

That distinction matters. It empowers all who understand the concept of Code-Shifting. Code-switching has a well-documented psychological cost: reduced authentic self-expression and increased stress.[ii]

When you can bring your full self into different spaces with awareness, you gain access without assimilation. You do not shrink. You translate. Leaders who can code-shift have a clear advantage in communicating well across all areas.

Digital Communication: Where Misunderstanding Lives

This is very important. Text messages and DMs are dangerous because tone is invisible. A survey of 2,000 adults found that 1/3 of people have fallen out with someone after misreading a text message.[iii] For young Black men and women, this can be costly.

Avoid texting during conflict. Avoid sarcasm in writing. Keep messages short and clear. Re-read before sending. When something feels complicated or emotional, call rather than text. Calling is always the better form of communication.

A short phone call can prevent misunderstandings that damage relationships, reputations, or opportunities. Digital maturity is part of communication intelligence.

HOW AUTHORITY FIGURES READ YOU

Coaches, teachers, managers, and employers are constantly asking silent questions: Are they coachable? Do they listen? Can they get feedback? Are they emotionally mature? Do they show respect? Are they reliable? Do they bring good energy?

Your communication answers all these questions every day.

Communicating With Confidence in Any Room

Confidence grows through action. Speak early in meetings or classrooms. Asking one thoughtful question establishes presence. Introduce yourself instead of waiting. Show gratitude; it signals leadership. Do not shrink your body or your voice. You belong.

Your Communication Is Your Passport

With strong communication, you can walk into classrooms, interviews, boardrooms, offices, and opportunities and walk out with respect and connection.

Communication changes how people see you.

Communication changes how people treat you.

Communication changes how you see yourself.

And when your communication is strong, doors don't just open, they stay open.

CHAPTER ASSIGNMENT: THE COMMUNICATION RESET

This week, complete the following:

1. **Craft and practice a 20-second introduction**
2. Include your name, role or school, interest or goal, and one personal detail. Say it out loud daily.
3. **Record yourself speaking for 30 seconds**
4. Watch posture, tone, eye contact, and pacing. Adjust intentionally.
5. **Give one genuine compliment each day**
6. Practice warmth and connection.

7. **Put your phone away during every conversation**
8. Presence alone will elevate your value.
9. **Speak confidently to one adult**
10. Teacher, coach, manager, or mentor. Practice calm, respectful communication.

Write down what felt different. Growth begins with awareness.

---

i. University of Houston. (2022). Do tattoos still carry a burden in today's workplace? UH News. https://stories.uh.edu/2022-tattoo-study/
ii. Dickens, D. D., Womack, V. Y., & Dimes, T. (2022). Social-cognitive and affective antecedents of code switching and the consequences of linguistic racism for Black people and other people of color. PMC/NCBI. https://pmc.ncbi.nlm.nih.gov/articles/PMC9382929/
iii. The Independent. (2021, September 10). A third of adults have fallen out with someone after misreading text messages, according to research. *The Independent.* https://www.the-independent.com/news/misreading-text-messages-research-adults-b1917768.html

TEN

How to Start Cold Conversations

WITHOUT FEAR OR AWKWARDNESS

If networking and people skills are the game, then cold conversations are the plays that win it. This is where the skill becomes real. This is where confidence stops being a motivational idea and becomes a decision you make with your feet, your voice, and your presence. A cold conversation is simply a conversation with someone you don't know yet, someone you haven't built a relationship with, someone who doesn't owe you anything, and someone who might have access to knowledge, opportunity, guidance, or connection. That "someone" could be a coach, a recruiter, a guest speaker, a professor, a business owner, an elder, a professional, or a potential mentor. It could be a manager at your job, a director at an internship fair, the person who just introduced themselves on stage, or the professional sitting quietly at the edge of the room. Cold conversations are how you turn strangers into resources and resources into relationships.

For many young people, especially African American students, walking into unfamiliar spaces, cold conversations can feel intimidating. Not because you lack intelligence. Not because you lack personality. But because of the invisible pressure that comes with being young and trying to be taken seriously or being Black in spaces where you might already feel watched, questioned, or underestimated. That pressure can make your brain do what it always does under stress: overthink. It starts by rehearsing every possibility. What if they ignore me? What if I sound dumb? What if I bother them? What if they judge me? What if I don't know how to keep it going? And just like that, the moment passes. The door stays closed. Not because it was locked, but because you never reached for the handle.

Here is the truth that can change your life: most opportunities you want are on the other side of one conversation you're afraid to start. You are not blocked by talent. You are not blocked by potential. You are not even blocked by a lack of access most of the time. More often than not, you are blocked by hesitation. Cold conversations open doors that talent alone never will. They create connections that applications cannot. They give you exposure that quiet excellence sometimes doesn't earn fast enough. They help people give your name a real personality. They allow adults to see your respect, your maturity, your curiosity, and your ambition, traits that matter just as much as skill.

Career development research backs this up. Students and young professionals who conduct informational interviews are significantly more likely to receive referrals, mentorship, and job opportunities than those who submit applications alone. A national survey from the National Association of Colleges and Employers found that informational interviews and proactive outreach improved employment outcomes more than GPA alone.[i] Other studies have shown that most professionals are willing to help when approached respectfully, and that over 70% would meet with a student who reaches out with genuine interest.[ii]

In other words, the advantage goes to the one who asks.

The point of this chapter is to decrease fear from the equation and replace it with a simple, repeatable process. You are going to learn how to approach anyone, anywhere, without awkwardness, because you will understand that cold conversations are not random. They are structured. They are learnable. They are practicing. Once you master them, you will never again feel powerless in a room full of opportunity.

WHY COLD CONVERSATIONS FEEL HARD (AND WHY THAT'S NORMAL)

Most people assume the problem is that they don't know what to say. That's rarely the real problem. The real problem is what you think will happen if you speak. Fear is not logical. Fear is protective. Fear tries to keep you safe from embarrassment, rejection, and discomfort. It whispers, "Stay quiet. Stay invisible. Don't take the risk." But the cost of that safety is your future. When you don't speak, you don't get seen. When you don't get seen, you don't get chosen. And in competitive environments, such as school, sports, scholarships, internships, and jobs, being unseen is one of the quickest ways to be overlooked.

People struggle with cold conversations because they worry about saying the wrong thing, sounding awkward, being judged, being ignored, bothering the person, or freezing in the middle of it. They imagine the worst-case scenario and treat it like it's guaranteed. But most adults, especially mature professionals, love it when young people approach them with respect and confidence. It signals initiative. It signals courage. It signals leadership. In fact, many adults are hoping a young person will approach them because it reminds them of themselves at that age. It makes them feel useful. It makes them feel honored. Most professionals don't take offense at respectful curiosity. It energizes them.

People don't judge you for speaking up as much as you think. They judge you for being silent when it matters. Silence reads as disinterest. Silence reads as insecurity. Silence reads as immaturity. Silence reads as someone who doesn't know how to move in professional spaces. Speaking respectfully reads as readiness.

The goal here isn't to become an extrovert. The goal is to become intentional. You don't have to talk to everybody, but you do have to learn how to talk to the right people at the right time, with the right energy. That skill is life-changing.

WHAT COLD CONVERSATION IS REALLY FOR?

The goal of a cold conversation is not to impress. It's not to brag. It's not to say something deep. And it's not to talk forever. The goal is simple: connect, be remembered, and follow up. That's it.

 Cold conversations are the spark. Follow-up is the flame.

A spark alone doesn't build anything unless you protect it, feed it, and return to it. That's why most students miss out on opportunities. They speak once, feel proud, and then disappear. They don't turn the moment into a relationship. Professionals can't help someone who vanishes. It's amazing, given current technology and the fact that everyone has a cellphone, how many people miss opportunities to build relationships by not following up.

Cold conversations do three important things at once. First, they introduce you as a real person, not just a name. Second, they show your character in a way a résumé can't. Third, they position you for future access, advice, opportunities, recommendations, internships, and introductions. A cold conversation is a bridge. You don't walk across it by staring at it. You walk across it by stepping onto it.

THE 5-SECOND RULE: THE CURE FOR OVERTHINKING

If you want to talk to someone, approach within five seconds. Not five minutes. Not after you rehearse a speech. Not after you find the "perfect time." Five seconds. That window matters because your brain will choose either action or fear. If you give fear time, it will talk you out of everything.

First thing…first…. When you introduce yourself, you most often say your first and last name, or say your last name and then say your first and last name. Good eye contact is a must.

"My name is Kester Crosse," or "My name is Crosse, Kester Crosse."

Let me share another pearl called the 5-second rule. The five-second rule is simple: see the moment, take a breath, smile lightly, step forward, and open your mouth. The courage comes after the movement. Confidence is not the requirement; it is the reward. You don't wait to feel ready. You act, and readiness shows up.

That is how confidence is built in real life: reps. Not vibes. Not quotes. Reps.

THE #1 SCRIPT: COMPLIMENT + INTRODUCTION

The most reliable cold conversation method is also the simplest: compliment + introduction. It works because it opens the person emotionally. A sincere compliment communicates respect and attention. Then your introduction gives structure. You are not invading their space. You are honoring them and stepping into a professional exchange.

"Hi, I just wanted to say I really liked what you said about _____. My name is _____. Nice to meet you."

Or:

"Excuse me, I really admire what you've accomplished. My name is _____, and I'd love to ask you a quick question."

This works because most adults like sincere respect. They stop. They smile. They open. Respect plus confidence equals access, and notice what makes it powerful: you are not asking for a job. You are not begging for anything. You are simply connecting, learning, and showing maturity.

At a campus job fair, a young woman named Taylor decided to use this exact approach. She noticed a recruiter from a major consulting firm finishing a conversation with another student. Her heart was beating fast, but she remembered the five-second rule and stepped forward anyway.

"Hi, I really liked what you shared about how your firm invests in training new analysts," she said. "My name is Taylor. I'm a junior majoring in business, and I am really interested in consulting. Would you mind if I asked you a quick question about how you got started?"

In that one moment, she did three things. She gave a specific compliment that proved she was listening. She introduced herself clearly. Then she asked a simple, respectful question. That is YES → ADD → ASK in real life. She said yes to what he had just shared, added one short detail about herself, and asked a follow-up question that invited him to talk.

The recruiter smiled, relaxed his shoulders, and gave her his full attention. He answered her question, asked her about her interests, and then suggested she apply for the firm's summer analyst program. Before she walked away, Taylor asked if she could connect with him on LinkedIn and follow up by email. That night, she sent a short message thanking him, mentioning one specific thing she learned, and letting him know she had started the application. A few weeks later, she was invited to interview and eventually earned an offer.

The cold conversation did not replace her résumé or her hard work, but it made sure her résumé was not just one of hundreds in a pile. It put a real person, a real voice, and a real presence behind her name. That is what cold conversations do when used well. They give your talent a chance to be seen.

COLD CONVERSATION THAT CHANGED MY LIFE

As a college junior at Hampton University, I was fortunate to be surrounded by several responsible friends who knew when it was time to study and were not afraid to say so. One of those friends was Dwayne Thompson. When others were choosing social time, Dwayne consistently chose preparation. More importantly, he reminded *me* of what I said I wanted: to go to medical school.

Choosing the right friends in college is a chapter unto itself, but Dwayne Thompson and Pat Ford are two examples of friends who led by example and helped keep me on track.

One day, Dwayne called me with critical information. A recruiter from the University of North Carolina School of Medicine was visiting the campus. He told me where and when.

I showed up immediately.

When I walked into the room, it was packed with people just like me: driven, African American students, smart, ambitious, and all wanting the same opportunity: a chance at medical school. I knew two things instantly. First, I *had* to meet this recruiter. Second, I needed him to *remember me.*

That meant I had to use cold conversation skills.

I positioned myself strategically in the room, listening while others spoke with him. As I waited, I noticed something important: the recruiter was wearing an Omega Psi Phi fraternity ring.

One of the most powerful principles of cold conversation is finding *one authentic point of connection.* Shared ground builds trust faster than credentials ever will.

When it was my turn, I introduced myself confidently. I spoke about his program details I had picked up by listening carefully to the conversations before mine. Then I mentioned my role model: my father, who was a member of Omega Psi Phi.

His face changed.

He told me his father was an Omega as well. I added that I also had two uncles who were members. The conversation shifted from transactional to personal in seconds.

He then asked me about my GPA. It was solid. He handed me his card and said, "Make sure you keep in touch and apply to my program."

This was 1991…no email, no cell phones.

I followed up with a letter thanking him for his time and formally applied to the summer program. I was accepted, and I was the *only* student from Hampton University to get in.

That summer program changed my life. It sharpened my focus, raised my expectations, and confirmed my path to medicine. I performed well, and later I was admitted to the University of North Carolina School of Medicine.

Hard work carried me through the program.

But a cold conversation *created the opportunity*.

Without good friends and without the ability to confidently connect with someone I had never met, I never would have gotten my foot in the door.

Seven Cold Conversation Starters You Can Use Anywhere

Cold conversation starters work best when they are short, respectful, and curiosity-based. The goal is to make the conversation easy for the other person to enter. You're not trying to be clever. You're trying to be clear.

1. You can start with an event-based question: "Hi, I'm _____. What brings you here today?" That works at networking events, college fairs, conferences, and even campus gatherings because it gives the person an easy answer.

2. You can show that you were paying attention: "I heard you mention _____. Can you say more about that?" This signals maturity because it proves you listen before you speak.
3. You can ask for advice: "I'm really interested in _____. Do you have any advice?" People love giving advice because it makes them feel useful and respected.
4. You can ask the question that creates mentors: "How did you get started in your career?" This question invites a story. Stories build connection.
5. You can ask for practical guidance: "I'm trying to learn more about _____. Any tips?" This communicates humility and hunger.
6. You can affirm their impact: "I appreciate what you said earlier. It made me think about _____." That makes you memorable because it proves you're thoughtful.
7. Or you can use the simplest permission opener: "Do you mind if I ask you a quick question?" Most people say yes because it feels respectful and low-pressure.

These starters aren't magic lines. They are doors. Your job is to walk through them with presence.

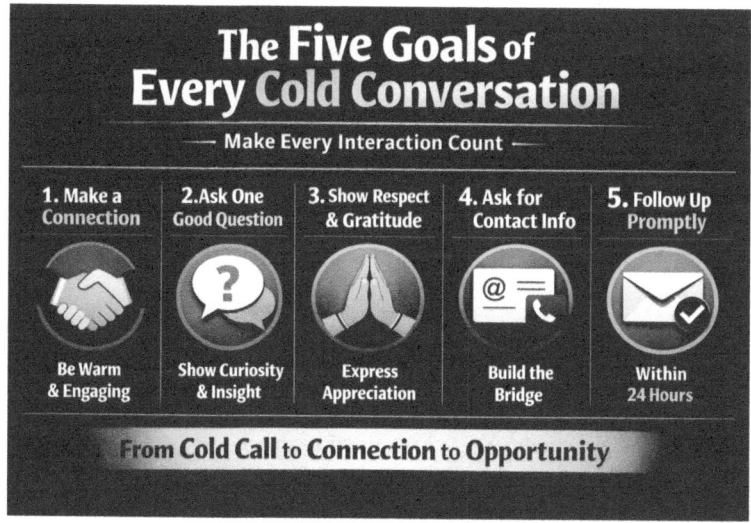

Figure 6: Effective Conversations

The Five Goals of Every Cold Conversation

A cold conversation doesn't need to be long. It needs to be effective. You can measure effectiveness by five goals.

First, make a connection. A warm approach always works. Warmth is a skill. It's eye contact, a smile, and a respectful tone.

Second, ask one good question. People remember good questions more than they remember your résumé. A good question shows curiosity, maturity, and intelligence. It also makes the other person feel valued.

Third, show respect and gratitude. Our culture understands this deeply. Elders notice gratitude instantly. Professionals notice it too. A simple "Thank you for your time" goes farther than you realize.

Fourth, ask for contact information when appropriate. This is the bridge to opportunity. If you don't ask, you leave the connection floating in the air where it usually disappears. You can say it smoothly: "Would it be okay if I stay in touch?" or "Could I connect with you by email?" It's respectful and direct.

Fifth, follow up within twenty-four hours. This is where most people fail. They feel proud that they talked, then they vanish. You won't. You will send the message that turns a moment into a relationship.

How to Close the Conversation Smoothly

Ending matters. A strong exit leaves a strong final impression. You don't drift away. You close with respect.

"Thanks again for speaking with me. May I stay in touch?"

"I appreciate your time. Can I connect with you by email or phone?"

"It was great meeting you. I hope our paths cross again."

Short. Polite. Clear. Nobody feels awkward. Everyone feels respected.

WHAT HAPPENS AFTER: TURNING A MOMENT INTO MENTORSHIP

After the first conversation, your goals shift. Now you're building a relationship. That means reinforcing the connection with a short thank-you message, highlighting something specific you learned, keeping it brief and respectful, and not asking for something big right away. Relationships grow. Don't rush.

You stay on their radar by sharing a small update occasionally: a goal you hit, a class you enjoyed, a scholarship you applied for, a lesson you used from their advice. Professionals love seeing growth because it proves their investment matters. This is how mentorship forms naturally. Mentorship is not forced. It is earned through consistency.

And remember, not everyone you meet becomes a mentor. Some become a contact. Some become a reference. Some become a future opportunity. Some become a bridge to someone else. The goal is not to squeeze every person for value. The goal is to build a network rooted in respect.

Quick ABC's for any Follow up Conversation for Relationship Building

1. Find out how their past weekend or some timeframe (month, week, past 6 months)
2. Share something positive about your past timeframe since you last connected
3. May discuss another topic about their life, and you share something.
4. Close out the conversation and set a tentative follow-up discussion.

Real Scripts You Can Copy (And Make Your Own)

When approaching a professional, you can say: "Hi, my name is _____. I really liked what you said about _____. I'm trying to learn more about that. Can I ask you a quick question?" That's clean, respectful, and confident.

At a networking event, you can say: "Hello, I'm _____. I don't think we've met yet. What brought you here today?" This is smooth and easy.

Talking to a coach can sound like: "Coach, I appreciate your time. Is there anything you think I should focus on to get better?" Coaches love this question because it shows humility and work ethic.

After an event, you can say: "Thank you for speaking today. Your story about _____ really inspired me. Could we stay connected?" That's memorable because it's specific.

Your follow-up message can be simple: "Hello _____, this is _____. Thank you again for your time yesterday. I really appreciated your insight about _____. I'd love to stay in touch." Keep it short. Professionals appreciate clarity.

Scripts aren't meant to make you robotic. They are training wheels. You use them until confidence becomes natural.

Why Adults Respect Young People Who Start Conversations

Adults love young people who start conversations because it signals initiative and courage. It signals professionalism and maturity. It signals humility, confidence, and leadership. It signals that you're not waiting to be chosen, you're preparing to earn it. Those are rare qualities. When adults see them, they want to help. They want to guide. They want to open doors.

People don't forget young people with presence.

Cold Conversations Are Courage in Action

Every door you want to open, every opportunity you want access to, every mentor you hope to meet, every connection that could change your life is one conversation away. When you combine your natural rhythm, cultural warmth, presence, and confidence, you become someone people want to talk to. Cold conversations aren't scary. They're powerful. They are not a personality trait. They are a skill.

And now you have the cheat codes.

Now it's time to run the play.

END-OF-CHAPTER ASSIGNMENT: THE COLD CONVERSATION CHALLENGE

This week, you will start a cold conversation. Not five. Not "someday." One.

Pick one person: a teacher, a coach, a counselor, a mentor, an older student who's doing well, or someone in your dream career. Use the five-second rule. Walk up with calm energy. Use a compliment plus an introduction. Ask one good question. Close respectfully. If it makes sense, ask for contact info.

Then follow up within twenty-four hours with a short message that includes three things: gratitude, one specific detail you learned, and a simple statement that you'd like to stay connected.

After you do it, write down what happened. What did you feel before you approached? What changed once you started speaking? What surprised you? What would you do differently next time? That reflection is how you turn one rep into a new level of confidence.

---

i. National Association of Colleges and Employers. (2024). Job Outlook 2024. NACE. https://www.naceweb.org/docs/default-source/default-document-library/2023/publication/research-report/2024-nace-job-outlook.pdf
ii. Keith Ferrazzi, *Never Eat Alone: And Other Secrets to Success, One Relationship at a Time* (New York: Crown Business, 2005).

ELEVEN

Career Pathways & Possibilities

SEEING BIGGER, REACHING FURTHER

At some point in life, every young person asks the same question: What should I do with my future? Some ask it with excitement because they can feel a possibility calling them. Some ask it with fear because the future feels like a fog, and nobody handed them a map. And some ask it because no one ever showed them what's available.

Too many young African American students ask that question while carrying invisible limits on their shoulders, limits they did not create but limits they must outgrow. I don't know anyone in that field. People like me don't usually do that. Nobody in my family did this. What if I'm not good enough? What if I fail? Those thoughts sound personal, but they are often inherited. They come from history, from a lack of exposure, from environments where survival was emphasized over exploration.

This chapter is here to shatter those limits, not with hype, but with clarity. The truth is simple, and it is bigger than your fear: you can do anything, you can become anything, and your story and your culture do not restrict you; they elevate you. The goal is not to pick a perfect career on your first try. The goal is to see wider, aim higher, and start walking with purpose instead of waiting for certainty.

WHAT IS YOUR CAREER CALLING?

Your career is more than a job. It is more than a paycheck. It is the place where your gifts, your story, and your discipline come together to serve others. That's why your calling matters. Calling doesn't have to be dramatic. It doesn't have to sound like something you announce on a stage. Your calling is simply what you feel pulled to do that also creates value in the world. When you find a path that fits your strengths and your values, work stops feeling like punishment and starts feeling like purpose, and for Black students, purpose has an extra layer of representation. The world needs Black doctors, Black lawyers, Black engineers, Black teachers, Black entrepreneurs, Black coaches, Black architects, Black pilots, Black scientists, Black tradesmen, Black technologists, Black leaders, Black thinkers, and Black creators. Representation isn't a slogan. It is a necessity. When people see you walk into a room confidently, you don't just change the space; you change expectations. You change what younger kids believe is possible. You change what patients feel when they're scared. You change what a company thinks leadership can look like. You change what the next generation imagines for themselves.

To understand why your career choices matter, you must understand what your family and community went through. For generations, our community had limited access to certain pathways, such as medical school, law, technology, corporate leadership, finance, engineering, and real estate development, not because we lacked intelligence or potential, but because we often lacked exposure, opportunity, and connections. You can't chase what you've never seen. You can't imagine what no one ever explained. But today, you are not starting from scratch. You are standing on the shoulders of people who sacrificed so you could choose your destiny. That's why your career matters. It's not just about you getting a job. It's about you carrying your family's legacy forward. It's about breaking barriers for those coming behind you. It's about expanding the image of Black excellence. It's about building generational wealth, yes, but also generational confidence. It's about becoming the mentor somebody else needs, the example somebody else follows, and the proof that "people like us" can do anything. Your success is not selfish when done with integrity; it is service.

One of the biggest problems young people face is thinking that careers are limited to what they see every day. If your neighborhood has teachers, nurses, retail workers, and a few business owners, you might assume those are the only lanes. That is not true. The world is filled with careers you have never heard of and roles you have never seen up close. That is why this chapter is about pathways and possibilities, not so you get overwhelmed, but so you stop thinking small. Healthcare is one obvious lane: nurses, physicians, therapists, technicians, administrators, researchers, and public health leaders. The medical field desperately needs more African American voices, not just for representation, but for trust. Imagine being the doctor who makes Black patients feel safe, understood, and respected. Imagine being the administrator who designs systems that treat people fairly. Imagine being the therapist who helps young men process life without shame. Healthcare is not just a job category. It is a mission field.

CAREER FIELDS TO EXPLORE

Engineering

Engineering is another lane that too many students overlook because it sounds intimidating. Mechanical, electrical, civil, and software engineers build the world. They design bridges, cars, apps, medical devices, and systems that keep society running. It is one of the most stable, respected, and well-paid fields, and it rewards problem solvers. If you like figuring things out, taking things apart mentally, building solutions, and thinking logically, engineering is a pathway worth exploring. And technology is the new frontier, not just for coders, but for cybersecurity, AI, data science, user experience design, project management, product development, and more. Many students do not realize this: you can learn to code through free and low-cost programs and build a career faster than people think. Tech rewards skill more than pedigree. It is one of the few spaces where a strong portfolio can compete with a famous name. If you build something real, people pay attention.

Business and Entrepreneurship

Business and entrepreneurship deserve deeper mention because entrepreneurship has always been part of Black culture, even when it was not celebrated. We have always created lanes when none existed. Owning a business changes a family's financial future because it shifts you from earning money to building something that generates money. Entrepreneurship can take many forms: real estate, logistics, marketing, a barbershop, a tech startup, a cleaning company, a healthcare practice, a clothing brand, or a financial services business. The details matter, but the principle is the same: ownership creates leverage. And business is not just about making money. It is about solving problems and creating value. If you want freedom, entrepreneurship is a powerful option, but it requires discipline, patience, and people skills at the highest level.

Law

Law is another field where representation has a real impact. Attorneys, judges, policy advisors, and civil rights advocates; these roles shape what justice looks like in real life. Our communities need legal advocates who understand the cultural context of what people face. A strong Black lawyer is not just building a career; they are often protecting families, defending futures, and expanding access. Education matters too. One great Black teacher can change hundreds of lives across decades. The impact multiplies. Teachers, professors, counselors, administrators: these are roles that shape students' confidence and identity. If you have ever had an educator who saw you clearly and pushed you upward, then you already understand how powerful that is.

Skilled Trades

Skilled trades are often overlooked because society sometimes treats them like "less than." That is ignorance. Electricians, plumbers, HVAC technicians, carpenters, and many of the highest-paying jobs in America are trades, and many of them come without the debt of college. Trades reward discipline, learning, and quality. Trade also creates entrepreneurial opportunities because skilled trades can lead to ownership quickly.

Finance

Finance is another lane that matters deeply for our community because understanding money is power. Banking, investing, real estate, wealth management, accounting, these pathways allow you to build wealth and help others do the same. When a Black professional understands finance, they can change entire family trees. And creative careers are real careers too: film, music, graphic design, photography, journalism, marketing, and content creation. Creativity can build a career when it is paired with discipline and strategy. Talent alone is not enough, but talent plus structure becomes profit.

Sports and Entertainment

Finally, sports-adjacent careers matter for athletes and sports lovers. Even if you do not go pro, you can stay in the world you love through athletic training, sports medicine, coaching, management, operations, analytics, broadcasting, and business roles inside athletics. Sports are a giant industry, not just a dream.

YOUR STORY IS YOUR ADVANTAGE

No matter what lane you choose, you need to understand something important: your story is an asset in every career. Your background, culture, community, and experiences can foster empathy, resilience, emotional intelligence, adaptability, communication skills, cultural awareness, and a work ethic. These traits are valuable everywhere. Never think your upbringing holds you back. It often gives you a perspective others do not have. Many professionals across industries say the same thing in different words: *I* hire for character. I can teach them skills. Skills can be trained. Character is harder to build.

Your character is your currency. Your reliability is your résumé. Your consistency is your reputation.

The Only Thing Constant is Change

Now, let us make career choices less stressful. Most young people feel pressure to pick a career as if it were a life sentence. It is not. Stop thinking about careers as "forever." Think about them as chapters. Your first career may not be your last. Your first major may not be your final identity. Many people pivot. Many people evolve. The goal is not to choose perfectly. The goal is to choose intentionally and start moving. That is why I use a simple formula: talent, passion, purpose, and pathway.

TALENT, PASSION, PURPOSE, AND PATHWAY

Figure 7: Your Career Sweetspot

Talent is what you are naturally good at or what you can become great at through effort. Ask yourself what feels natural and what people compliment you on. **Passion** is what energizes you. What do you enjoy learning about? What topics make time move fast? **Purpose** is what matters to you. What impact do you want to have? What problem do you care about solving? **Pathway** is practical. What opportunities are available? What can get you into a career without a twenty-year delay? What path can you grow into? Where can you build wealth? When you combine talent, passion, purpose, and pathway, you find your career sweet spot. And you can revisit that sweet spot as you mature, gain exposure, and learn more about yourself.

MENTORSHIP MATTERS

One of the most powerful accelerators of career success is mentorship.[i] Mentorship is the shortcut nobody wants to admit is real. The direct route to career clarity is simple: find someone who has done what you want to do and learn from them. Mentors open doors. Mentors warn you about mistakes. Mentors guide you through challenges. Mentors give you confidence. Mentors answer questions that Google cannot answer because they come from experience. For Black students especially, mentors are life-changing because they do not just teach skills; they teach navigation. They show you what is possible. They give you the playbook. They can speak into your life with cultural understanding. They help you move through spaces where you may be the only one. And if you do not have a mentor yet, you already learned how to start building that network in the previous chapter. Cold conversations are not just networking; they are mentorship auditions. Every respectful introduction is a seed.

Your Career is Bigger than You

That is not pressure, it's purpose. When you build a strong career, you uplift your family. You inspire siblings and cousins. You influence your circle. You shift expectations. You change what the next generation believes is possible. You become the blueprint. That is what parents and grandparents prayed for, not just that you would survive, but that you would have choices. Not just that you would make money, but that you would build stability and freedom. Not just that you would succeed, but that you would become someone others can follow.

But you do not reach that future by thinking about it forever. You reach it by taking the next step. Big dreams require small moves. Career success is not one decision. It is a series of courageous decisions. It is learning yourself. It is seeking exposure. It is asking questions. It is testing interests. It is building skills. It is being coachable. It is being consistent. It is doing the work before you feel fully ready.

END-OF-CHAPTER ASSIGNMENT: IDENTIFY YOUR NEXT STEP

Take ten minutes today and answer these questions on paper, not in your head.

First, list three careers that interest you right now. Do not overthink it. Pick any combination: medicine, business, trades, tech, law, sports-adjacent careers, education, creative work, finance, engineering, anything. The goal is to name possibilities, not to commit to life.

Second, identify one adult who is doing something you would like to learn more about. One person. It could be a teacher, a coach, a family friend, a professional at church, an alum, a neighbor, or someone you meet at an event. Your job this week is to reach out with a respectful message and ask one question about their path.

Third, write down one skill you can start developing right now that will serve you in any career. Communication, professionalism, time management, coding, writing, public speaking, financial literacy, interviewing, networking, pick one and commit to improving it for thirty days.

Fourth, name one fear you need to release. Write it honestly: I am not smart enough. I might fail. This is not for people like me. I do not know anyone. I am behind. Then write a response to that fear as if you are coaching yourself: I can learn. I can grow. I can ask. I can practice. I can build. I can start.

Your career begins with awareness, but it grows through action. One brave step can change everything.

You do not need permission to become great. The world may not always make space for you, but you can create your own space. Your career possibilities are endless. Your story is powerful. Your culture is a strength. Your presence is needed. You are the future doctor, engineer, teacher, leader, business owner, lawyer, creator, or innovator someone is praying for. Your purpose is bigger than your fear. Your destiny is bigger than your doubt. Your future is bigger than your circumstances. The world is ready for you.

Now it is time for you to be ready for it.

---

i. Harker, A., & Shanks, R. (2024). The impact of mentoring in higher education on student career development: A systematic review and research agenda. Studies in Higher Education. https://doi.org/10.1080/03075079.2024.2354894

TWELVE

Running the Play

PUTTING IT ALL TOGETHER

You've learned the skills. You've seen the examples. You've practiced the strategies. You've built the mindset. Now it's time to run the play. That phrase matters because life is not a classroom where you get credit for what you "understand." Life rewards what you apply. Information is useless without action. Potential is nothing without execution. Even the best playbook in the world won't win you a game if you never step on the court. This chapter is the closing whistle and the locker-room talk at the same time. It pulls everything together with your story, your people skills, your work ethic, your communication, your professionalism, your presence, and your purpose, and it puts it into motion. If the earlier chapters taught you what to do, this one teaches you how to live it daily, how to build a repeatable system, and how to become the kind of person opportunity recognizes.

Most people get inspired, then they go back to life as usual. They read a book, they highlight a paragraph, they feel motivated for a day, and then the old habits return like gravity.

That's not because they're lazy; it's because they don't have a system.

WHAT IS GREATNESS?

Greatness is not a personality trait. It's a pattern. It's what you repeatedly do when no one is clapping. That's why athletes are such powerful role models. Athletes don't win because they get "inspired" on game day. They won because they practiced when it wasn't exciting. They ran drills when nobody watched. They built habits that show up under pressure. That is what this book has been building toward: turning your people skills into a habit, turning your discipline into a lifestyle, and turning your confidence into something that doesn't depend on the room you walk into.

The Final Truth

Let's start with the truth that should free you: you do not need to master everything at once. **You need to master the next thing.** You don't become an elite communicator overnight. You build reps. You don't become a powerful networker overnight. You build relationships. You don't become "high market value" by wishing it into existence. You build consistency. That is the idea behind running the play. You take what you learned, and you run it in real situations—classrooms, locker rooms, campuses, workplaces, family events, churches, conferences, offices, interviews, and everyday conversations. The play is not a theory. The play is behavior.

How the Earlier Chapters Fit the Play

- **Chapter 1** reframed history as something you write through daily decisions. People skills open doors talent can't, and running the play starts with responsibility for how you show up.
- **Chapter 2** showed discipline as an inheritance and warned against wasted talent. You are connected to generations of resilience and grit; running the play honors that lineage by developing your gifts rather than becoming another "almost" story.
- **Chapter 3** addressed phone etiquette and presence — early, because it is the first daily test of discipline. In a world of distraction, presence is currency, especially for young Black professionals who are judged quickly and often unfairly. Professionalism becomes protection, and presence becomes the foundation on which everything else is built.
- **Chapter 4** turned your story into your résumé. Leaders introduce themselves with clarity. When someone asks, "Tell me about yourself," you don't shrink — you communicate identity and direction.
- **Chapter 5** introduced the TEEE Score — Talent, Effort, Energy, Execution, and why reliability outruns raw talent. Raising your baseline makes you the one teachers recommend, coaches trust, and managers invest in.
- **Chapter 6** expanded market value beyond money. Value is built through choices: arrival time, follow-up, listening, emotional control, and integrity. Your reputation forms long before your résumé is read.
- **Chapter 7** demystified networking. Relationships aren't random; they're bridges. Visibility, likability, and trust equal access.

- **Chapter 8** justified small talk. It's not about the topic; it's the warm-up that makes deeper relationships possible.
- **Chapter 9** sharpened communication. Clarity is not imitation; it's preparation. You learned to be heard without being loud and respected without being aggressive.
- **Chapter 10** broke down cold conversations and follow-up. Confidence is usually the reward for action, not the prerequisite.
- **Chapter 11** expanded career imagination. Careers are built through exposure, skill-building, mentorship, and steps — not perfect planning.

Run Winning Plays in Life

So, what does "running the play" look like in real life? It looks like waking up with intention. It looks like simple habits repeated daily that raise your market value over time. It looks like practicing your introduction until it's clean. It looks like speaking early in rooms instead of hiding. It looks like being the first to shake hands, the first to say hello, and the first to send the follow-up message. It looks like walking into a room as if you belong without needing permission. It looks like being present enough to notice who is alone and including them. It looks like being disciplined enough to put your phone away even when your friends can't. It looks like being mature enough to control your emotions even when you feel disrespected. It looks like remembering that your long-term goals are bigger than your temporary feelings.

WHY DO MOST PEOPLE FAIL?

Most people fail not because they lack ability, but because they lack consistency. They do the right thing "sometimes," and they call it effort. But effort that shows up only when you feel like it is not effort, it's mood. Leaders can't trust moods. Coaches can't build around moods. Success belongs to the person who can execute regardless of mood. That's why execution is the step most people never take. They love to plan. They love to talk. They love to dream. But when it's time to do the boring work practice, repetition, follow-up, discipline, they disappear. You won't. You can't afford to. Not because you're trying to prove something to anyone, but because you owe it to yourself and to the future you're building.

The Cultural Edge

There is also an African American advantage that the world cannot teach. You have rhythm. You have resilience. You have emotional intelligence built from reading rooms your whole life. You have warmth. You have presence. You have creativity. You have grit. You have leadership instincts. You have adaptability. You have culture. You have community. These traits make you magnetic when they are paired with professionalism and discipline. People are drawn to authenticity with maturity. They are drawn to confidence without arrogance. They are drawn to energy that feels both safe and strong. When you combine your cultural strengths with trained communication and consistent execution, you become unstoppable. Your ancestors survived so you could succeed. Your elders sacrificed so you could dream. Your community prays for your growth. You are your ancestors' wildest dreams. Now it's your turn to dream even bigger and then do the work that matches that dream.

BECOME THE PERSON PEOPLE SAY "YES" TO

Becoming the person people say "yes" to is not about manipulation or popularity. It's about trust. It's about becoming dependable. It's about being a person who makes other people's lives easier, not harder. It's about being the person who listens, because people trust listeners. It's about being the person who follows up, because most young people don't, and that alone separates you. It's about being the person who shows respect, because respect opens doors, pride keeps them closed. It's about being the person who asks questions, because questions show intelligence and humility. It's about being humble and hungry, because confidence without arrogance is power. It's about knowing your story, because your story is your introduction to the world. It's about bringing good energy, because your energy becomes your reputation before your résumé is ever read. When you consistently embody these traits, people want to help you. They want to mentor you. They want to invest in you. They want to connect you. You become the young person everyone roots for, not because you begged for it, but because you earned it.

The Village is Watching

Excellence is not a solo sport. It's a team effort. A community effort. A "we-before-me" effort. Your little cousins are watching. Your siblings are watching. Your teammates are watching. Your neighborhood is watching. Your future children are watching. You are inspiring people you don't even know. Your success becomes a light others follow. That's why running the play matters. Not because you must carry the world, but because your life can become proof. Proof that discipline works. Proof that communication matters. Proof that presence changes outcomes. Proof that a young person can be both culturally authentic and professionally excellent.

A REPEATABLE SYSTEM

That is why we end with a checklist, not as a cute ending, but as a life tool.

Daily, speak confidently. Make eye contact. Put your phone away in conversations. Ask one good question. Do one thing that improves your future.

Weekly, start a new conversation. Follow up with one mentor, teacher, or coach. Practice your introduction. Declutter your social media. Learn something new through a book, a podcast, a YouTube lesson, or a skill course.

Monthly, set goals. Reflect on growth. Adjust habits. Update your network. Celebrate small wins. Do that for twelve months, and you will not recognize your life, because you'll have built a new identity, an identity rooted in action.

Focus Forward

I have always been inspired by the 10 two-letter words regarding success. The 10 words are this…" **If it is to be, it is up to me!**"

You are ready, but readiness isn't a feeling. It's a decision. You have the playbook. You have the mindset. You have the skills. You have the story. You have the culture. You have discipline. You have confidence. You have the purpose. Now it's time to become the person you were created to be: a leader, a connector, a communicator, a professional, a role model, a door-opener, a barrier-breaker, a success-maker. Open doors for yourself. Open doors for others. Open doors for generations. Because the world needs your voice. The world needs your gifts. The world needs your story. The world needs your excellence. And now you have everything you need to walk through every open door with confidence, courage, and purpose.

END-OF-CHAPTER ASSIGNMENT: RUN THE PLAY FOR 14 DAYS

For the next fourteen days, you are going to stop "consuming" information and start living it. Your assignment is simple: run the play daily and track it like a scoreboard. Each day, complete the five actions below and give yourself one point for each. Your goal is not perfection; your goal is consistency. If you miss a day, don't quit. Reset the next day. Champions don't win because they never fail; they win because they don't stop.

Each day for 14 days:

1. **Presence Point:** Have one conversation with your phone fully out of reach. Not face-up. Not in your hands. Away.
2. **Communication Point:** Speak up once in a space where you normally stay quiet. Ask a question, contribute a thought, or introduce yourself.
3. **Connection Point:** Start one small conversation; small talk counts. Use YES → ADD → ASK or one FROM question.
4. **Follow-Up Point:** Send one message that strengthens a relationship—thank you, a check-in, appreciation, an update, or a quick question.
5. **Discipline Point:** Do one thing today that improves your future: study, work out, read 10 pages, practice

your intro, apply for something, research a career, or learn a skill.

At the end of the 14 days, write one paragraph answering these:

- What felt easiest and why?
- What felt hardest and why?
- What changed in your confidence?
- What changed in how people responded to you?
- What is one habit you will keep for the next 90 days?

This is how you close the gap between potential and purpose.

This is how you stop being "almost."

This is how you build a reputation that opens doors before you even knock.

This is how you run the play until the play becomes your lifestyle—and your lifestyle becomes your life advantage.

Key Terms

FRAMEWORKS & METHODS

5-Second Rule (Chapter 10)

A technique for overcoming hesitation in cold conversations: when you see someone you want to meet, approach within five seconds before your brain generates excuses. Confidence comes after movement, not before.

Compliment + Introduction (Chapter 10)

The most reliable cold conversation opener: offer a sincere compliment, then introduce yourself clearly. Example: "I really liked what you said about _____. My name is _____. Nice to meet you."

Four Levels of Communication (Chapter 8)

The dimensions of how we communicate: Verbal (words and clarity), Non-Verbal (body language and presence), Emotional (the energy you bring), and Cultural (navigating different environments authentically).

FROM Method (Chapter 7)

A conversation framework for building rapport using four topic areas: From/Family (where someone is from or their loved ones), Recreation (hobbies and interests), Occupation (work or field of study), and Motivation (what drives them).

TEEE Score (Chapter 5)

A four-factor assessment framework for measuring professional value: Talent (what you can do), Effort (how hard you work when no one is watching), Energy (how you make people feel), and Execution (your ability to deliver results). Scoring: 32-40 = Very Good; 20-31 = Average; Below 20 = Needs Work.

Three-Part Story (Chapter 4)

A framework for articulating your personal narrative: Past (where you come from and what shaped you), Present (who you are now and what you're building), Purpose (where you're going and why it matters).

YES → ADD → ASK (Chapter 8)

A three-step small talk technique: YES (acknowledge what was said), ADD (contribute one related thought), ASK (follow up with a question). Creates conversational rhythm without interrogation or monologue.

CORE CONCEPTS

Code-Shifting (Chapter 9)

Adapting your communication style across different environments while maintaining your authentic identity. Reframe: "I am skilled enough to communicate effectively across environments while remaining myself." Contrast with code-switching, which implies becoming someone else to be accepted.

Code-Switching (Chapter 9)

Changing how you speak, act, or present yourself to fit into different environments—often at the cost of feeling inauthentic. The mindset: "I have to become someone else to be accepted."

Cold Conversation (Chapter 10)

A conversation with someone you don't yet know—someone who doesn't owe you anything but may have access to knowledge, opportunity, guidance, or connection. The bridge between strangers and relationships.

Emotional Intelligence (EQ) (Chapters 1, 3)

The ability to recognize, understand, manage, and effectively use emotions in yourself and others. The engine behind self-awareness, discipline, regulation, and intentional action in professional and personal settings.

Market Value (Chapter 5)

How others perceive your worth based on daily choices, habits, emotional regulation, and presence—not salary or titles. Market value is built through consistency and shaped by how people remember you when you're not in the room.

People Skills (Chapter 1)

The ability to connect, communicate, and build relationships that open doors. Also called "soft skills" or "power skills." Unlike talent, people skills can be learned by anyone and often determine who gets chosen over who gets noticed.

Presence (Chapters 3, 6, 8)

The energy, attention, and awareness you bring into a space. Demonstrated through eye contact, body language, phone-free engagement, and calm confidence. Presence is noticed before credentials are verified.

Small Talk (Chapter 7)

The warm-up conversation is before deeper relationships become possible. Not about the topic, but about creating comfort and connection. Small talk is how people decide whether to lean in or pull back.

BEHAVIORS & ATTRIBUTES

Coachability (Chapter 6)

The willingness to receive feedback, adjust behavior, and improve without defensiveness. One of the key behaviors that raises market value and builds trust with mentors and leaders.

Effort (Chapter 5)

How hard do you work when no one is watching? The discipline to practice, push through discomfort, and show up consistently without external validation.

Energy (Chapter 5)

How you make people feel through your attitude, enthusiasm, and emotional presence. High-energy individuals lift rooms; low-energy individuals drain them regardless of talent.

Execution (Chapter 5)

The ability to deliver results under real-world conditions. Finishing strong, meeting deadlines, following through, and performing under pressure. Where credibility is built or lost.

Follow-Up (Chapters 7, 10)

The act of reconnecting after an initial meeting or conversation—typically within 24 hours. Includes expressing gratitude, mentioning a specific detail discussed, and stating a desire to stay connected. "Cold conversations are the spark. Follow-up is the flame."

CULTURAL & CONTEXTUAL TERMS

Black Conversation (Chapter 8)

A cultural superpower rooted in African American traditions of storytelling, connection, reading energy, and making people feel seen. Skills developed through barbershop debates, family cookouts, and community gatherings can be translated into professional settings.

Phubbing (Chapter 3)

The act of snubbing someone in favor of your phone during a conversation. A market value killer that signals "you're not important" to the other person.

The Exposure Gap (Prologue)

The disadvantage faced by young people—especially first-generation students and those from underrepresented backgrounds—who lack access to professional networks, unwritten rules of success, and mentorship that others receive naturally. (Prologue)

The Village (Chapters 2, 12)

A cultural reference to the African American community network—family, mentors, elders, and community members who watch, invest in, and advocate for young people. "The village is watching" means your reputation is being built through observed behavior.

SUCCESS PRINCIPLES

Reps Practice repetitions (Chapter 10)

The idea that confidence and skill are built through repeated action, not motivation or inspiration. "That is how confidence is built in real life: reps. Not vibes. Not quotes. Reps."

Talent Opens the First Door. (Chapter 1)

The principle that raw ability gets you noticed initially, but people skills, consistency, and character determine whether subsequent doors open. "Talent might get you noticed. People skills get you chosen."

The 14-Day System (Chapter 12)

A comprehensive daily practice plan for implementing the book's principles: Presence Point, Story Point, Connection Point, Follow-Up Point, and Discipline Point—repeated for two weeks to build habits.

Afterword

GRATITUDE, GRACE, AND THE GIFT OF RELATIONSHIPS

As I close this book, I want to pause and acknowledge the people, places, and blessings that shaped me into the man I am today. None of this, my career, my growth, my purpose, or these pages would exist without God's guidance and the people He placed in my life. First, I thank God for covering me, for guiding my steps, for opening doors I didn't even know to knock on, and for giving me strength when I felt weak, wisdom when I felt lost, and purpose when I needed direction. Every achievement in my life reflects His grace, not my own greatness, and I never want to forget that the same hand that lifted me can lift anyone who stays faithful, focused, and willing to grow.

I also thank my parents and my family, who poured into me long before I understood the value of their lessons. Every sacrifice, every correction, every hug, every expectation, those were not random moments; they were the foundation. Family is the first classroom for character, and I am grateful for the love, structure, and identity they gave me. I'm grateful for the way family teaches you who you are before the world has a chance to label you, and for the way it reminds you that you come from something bigger than yourself. I carry those lessons into every room I walk into, and I've tried to pass them forward in every chapter of this book.

To my earliest friendships, especially from Haynes Park in Wilmington, Delaware, thank you. Those streets taught me how to compete, how to laugh, how to stand up for myself, and how to move with both confidence and humility. Long before I had professional titles, I learned loyalty, resilience, and the kind of toughness that comes from real life. Those friendships gave me a sense of belonging and sharpened my instincts, and I'm grateful for every conversation, every lesson, and every moment that helped shape me into someone who could keep going when life got heavy. Rick, Tony, Phil, Matt, Monty, Burnell, and Jon—just to name a few—are lifelong friends from those early days.

Hampton University is where I truly grew up. Hampton sharpened my mind, expanded my worldview, and connected me to lifelong friendships and a standard of excellence that still lives in me today. It gave me mentors who believed in a community that held me accountable, people who pushed me and corrected me, encouraged me, and reminded me that greatness is not a wish; it's a decision. Hampton didn't just educate me; it transformed me, and I will always be grateful for the way that institution shaped my confidence, discipline, and sense of purpose. Special thanks to Clay and Pat.

Working for decades in gastroenterology, caring for complex and vulnerable patients, taught me the meaning of service. Medicine humbled me, stretched me, and required a level of empathy and resilience I didn't know I had. Every patient, every difficult case, every late night, and every breakthrough reinforced the truth that healing is not just a profession; it is a calling. It reminded me that people skills aren't optional in life; they are essential. In healthcare, you don't just treat symptoms, you earn trust, you calm fear, you communicate hope, and you show up for people when they are at their most human. That experience deepened my belief that relationships and communication are not "extra." They are everything. Life friends Dr. Howell, Dr. Peter Darwin, Dr. Susan Wolfsthal, Dr. Frank Calia, Dr. Riba Kelsey, Dr. Mallory Williams, Dr. Jamokay Taylor, and Dr. Gavin Henry are just a few of the people who have had a positive impact on my life.

Being a member of Kappa Alpha Psi Fraternity, Inc. is one of the great honors of my life. The bond, the brotherhood, and the commitment to upholding those principles strengthened my character and my responsibility to uplift others. Kappa challenged me to lead, mentor, represent something bigger than myself, and be a man who makes a difference in the lives of those around him. Brotherhood taught me what this book teaches: your name means something, your presence matters, and your choices can open doors not just for you but for those who come behind you. Kappa brought me brothers for life.

And to my smart, beautiful, steady, and loving wife, Kisa Crosse, thank you. You are my partner, my peace, my balance, and my blessing. Your love grounds me. Your belief in me strengthens me. Your wisdom shapes me. You make every chapter of my life better, and I thank God for giving me someone worthy to build a life with. You remind me that success without love is empty, and that the greatest "achievement" a man can have is building a home filled with respect, laughter, loyalty, and grace.

As I reflect on the journey behind me and the purpose ahead, I've come to understand the true meaning of life: meaningful relationships and meaningful moments. Not titles. Not trophies. Not accolades. Not bank accounts. But people. But love. But memories. But purpose. But connection. From Wilmington to Hampton, from medicine to mentorship, from fraternity brotherhood to family leadership, from childhood lessons to adult responsibilities, these people and places shaped me, sharpened me, blessed me, and prepared me to pour into the next generation. If anything in this book helps a young person open a door, build a relationship, or believe in their own greatness a little more, then my journey has not been in vain. To God be the glory. To my family, my friends, my community, my fraternity, and my wife, "thank you."

You helped form me into the man I am today, and now it's my turn to help others do the same. I work to make others better. That's my goal, and I will die trying to do this every day.

End Book Review

Closing Reflection

Throughout this book, Dr. Kester Crosse has emphasized a central principle: professional success is not determined by talent alone. It is shaped by how you think, how you communicate, how you build relationships, and how intentionally you develop yourself over time.

If *Open Doors* has provided value to you, consider taking a moment to leave a brief review on **Amazon**. Your review helps other readers discover the book and supports the mission of equipping young professionals with the mindset and skills needed to grow, lead, and succeed.

If you would like to stay connected with Dr. Crosse and access additional insights, resources, and updates on future books, visit the author website at **drcrosseauthor.com**. The site offers ongoing guidance and tools designed to help professionals continue developing the skills and mindset discussed throughout this book.

Thank you for investing your time in this journey. Keep learning, keep growing, and keep opening doors—for yourself and for others.

About the Author

Kester Irwin Hanley Crosse II, MD is a physician, business leader, mentor, and speaker committed to helping young people develop the people skills that open doors long before résumés are read. A board-certified gastroenterologist with decades of experience in medicine and healthcare leadership, Dr. Crosse has evaluated, hired, coached, and mentored hundreds of students, athletes, and professionals across academic, corporate, and clinical settings.

A graduate of Hampton University and the University of Maryland School of Medicine, Dr. Crosse combines lessons from sports, leadership, culture, and emotional intelligence to teach what schools rarely do: how to communicate with confidence, build authentic relationships, navigate professional spaces, and become someone people trust and invest in.

Through mentorship, speaking, and writing, he is especially passionate about equipping African American students and young professionals with the skills to compete, connect, and lead in any room they enter without losing their identity. His work centers on one belief: talent opens the first door, but people skills open every door after that.

Dr. Crosse lives with his wife and family and is deeply involved in service, mentorship, and community leadership.

References

Dickens, D. D., Womack, V. Y., & Dimes, T. (2022). Social-cognitive and affective antecedents of code switching and the consequences of linguistic racism for Black people and other people of color. PMC. https://pmc.ncbi.nlm.nih.gov/articles/PMC9382929/

Duckworth, A. (2016). Grit: The power of passion and perseverance. Scribner.

Ernst & Young & espnW. (2022). Where will you find your next leader? The case for athlete-inspired leadership. EY Global. https://www.ey.com/en_au/athlete-programs/why-a-female-athlete-should-be-your-next-leader

Ferrazzi, K. (2005). Never eat alone: And other secrets to success, one relationship at a time. Crown Business.

Forrier, A., De Cuyper, N., & Akkermans, J. (2024). The role of social capital in employability models: A systematic review. Sustainability, 17(5), 1782. https://www.mdpi.com/2071-1050/17/5/1782

Goleman, D. (1995). Emotional intelligence: Why it can matter more than IQ. Bantam Books.

Harker, A., & Shanks, R. (2024). The impact of mentoring in higher education on student career development: A systematic review and research agenda. Studies in Higher Education. https://doi.org/10.1080/03075079.2024.2354894

Jeske, D., & Shultz, K. S. (2023). Tools, potential, and pitfalls of social media screening: Social profiling in personnel selection. Journal of Management, 49(7), 2391–2421. https://doi.org/10.1177/10506519231199478

Kadylak, T., Makki, T. W., Francis, J., Cotten, S. R., Rikard, R. V., & Sah, Y. J. (2022). Feeling ostracized by others' smartphone use: The effect of "phubbing" on social interaction. PMC. https://pmc.ncbi.nlm.nih.gov/articles/PMC9285876/

Methot, J. R., Rosado-Solomon, E. H., Downes, P. E., & Gabriel, A. S. (2021). Office chitchat as a social ritual: The uplifting yet distracting effects of daily small talk at work. Academy of Management Journal, 64(5), 1445–1471. https://doi.org/10.5465/amj.2018.1474

Mobley, S. D., & Johnson, J. M. (2024). The HBCU advantage: Reimagining social capital among students at historically Black colleges and universities. Frontiers in Education, 9, 1344073. https://doi.org/10.3389/feduc.2024.1344073

National Association of Colleges and Employers. (2024). Job outlook 2024.

NACE. https://www.naceweb.org/docs/default-source/default-document-library/2023/publication/research-report/2024-nace-job-outlook.pdf

Pirsoul, T., Parmentier, M., & Nils, F. (2023). Emotional intelligence and career-related outcomes: A meta-analysis. Human Resource Management Review, 33(3), 100967. https://doi.org/10.1016/j.hrmr.2023.100967

Suárez-Albanchez, J., Gutiérrez-Broncano, S., Jiménez-Estévez, P., & Palacios-Florencio, B. (2023). Emotional intelligence, leadership, and work teams: A hybrid literature review. Heliyon, 9(10), e20356. https://doi.org/10.1016/j.heliyon.2023.e20356

The Independent. (2021, September 10). A third of adults have fallen out with someone after misreading text messages, according to research. *The Independent.* https://www.the-independent.com/news/misreading-text-messages-research-adults-b1917768.html

University of Houston. (2022). Do tattoos still carry a burden in today's workplace? UH News. https://stories.uh.edu/2022-tattoo-study/

Zippia Career Research. (2023). Employee referral statistics: How referrals impact hiring. Zippia Research. https://www.zippia.com/advice/employee-referral-statistics/

Made in the USA
Columbia, SC
21 March 2026